Virtues and Vices

Virtues and Vices

STORIES OF THE MORAL LIFE

Andrew M. Greeley
Jacob Neusner
Mary Greeley Durkin

Westminster John Knox Press
Louisville, Kentucky

© 1999 Andrew M. Greeley, Jacob Neusner, and Mary Greeley
Durkin

Quotations from the Gospels are from the *Good News Bible*,
Today's English Version—New Testament, © American Bible
Society 1966, 1971, 1976, 1992.

Book design by Rohani Design, Edmonds, Washington
Cover design by Paz Design Group

Published by Westminster John Knox Press
Louisville, Kentucky

This book is printed on acid-free paper that meets the
American National Standards Institute Z39.48 standard. ∞

PRINTED IN THE UNITED STATES OF AMERICA

99 00 01 02 03 04 05 06 07 08 — 10 9 8 7 6 5 4 3 2 1

Library of Congress Cataloging-in-Publication Data

Greeley, Andrew M., 1928–
    Virtues and vices : stories of the moral life / Andrew M.
Greeley, Jacob Neusner, and Mary Greeley Durkin. — 1st ed.
        p.   cm.
    ISBN 0-664-22113-0 (alk. paper)
    1. Cardinal virtues. 2. Deadly sins. 3. Christian ethics—
Catholic authors. 4. Aggada—Translations into English.
5. Legends, Jewish. 6. Ethics, Jewish. I. Neusner, Jacob,
1932–   . II. Durkin, Mary Greeley. III. Title.
BV4645.G74 1999
241'.3—dc21   98-52754

Contents

Preface

Theological dialogue underscores the differences between Judaism and Christianity, because that dialogue makes both sides wonder how God can have delivered so many conflicting messages. But in North America and Western Europe, where sizable populations practice Judaism and where Christianity—Catholic, Protestant, and Orthodox—flourishes as well, people yearn to know one another and to work together for the greater glory of God. We live in an age of Judaic and Christian encounter in quest for amity and in the pursuit of common purpose in the service of humanity in God's image, after God's likeness. If the Holocaust precipitated the encounter in earnest, the half-century since has shown how much we may hope in the nurturing friendship between our long-divided but kindred faiths.

But taking the first steps toward one another proves difficult for the many who fiercely affirm the truths of their respective faiths. How, without negotiating truth, are we to form attitudes and feelings of sympathy for one another, and where shall we find the source of empathy that will make possible shared affirmation of common humanity before the One God? The three partners in this book work together to find stories that speak on the same ethical issues—matters of vice and virtue—for Catholic Christianity and Rabbinic Judaism, respectively. We identify in stories the bridge that we seek from heart to heart. And in these pages we further propose that, when each religion speaks of vice and virtue, it enters that orbit of common humanity before God that guides the journey through time and eternity of the other as well. Theological dialogue divides, but theological story-telling overcomes division. That is the conviction that we mean to express in this anthology of tales of how not to behave and how to live.

Do the Torah and Christ speak to the same humanity? They address in common the existential challenges of living life under God, one God, the only God, the same God for us all. They share fundamental assumptions, such as, in the words of Walter Moberly: "the dignity of human life, the centrality of love, trust, obedience, mercy, forgiveness; the living of the life of faith in community; prayer as the essential medium between God and humanity."[1]

To tales told from heart to heart men and women who practice Judaism or Christianity do respond, as deep calls to deep: we can respond to the art and narrative poetry of the other, the yearning for God conveyed by the other, the love of God that nourishes the other, shared in stories of real people, living out their years in this life. And here we mean to show, when the Catholic tells Catholic stories of moral conduct, when the Rabbinic sages record their narratives of exemplary conduct, they turn out to tell the same story in different garb.

These stories we mean to contribute, in their pairs—the Catholic, the rabbinic—like the animals in Noah's ark that saved life on earth, to the common dialogue. Should we lose all this, in the name of theological disputation? On the contrary, we propose to find in the stories we tell ourselves the face and form of the other portrayed in the story that the other tells too—on the very same issue of everyday conduct. It is toward a Judeo-Christian dialogue of quest, each in search of a tale to convey the authentic humanity of the other, that events of this awful century have brought us. It is time. And there is no other way.

---

1. Personal letter, August 8, 1991.

The Christian stories are told by Father Greeley, the Judaic ones are chosen and translated from the original Hebrew of the documents of the oral Torah by Rabbi Neusner out of the authoritative sources of rabbinic Judaism. The sets of stories could not begin at more remote places of time and space. But that makes the outcome all the more remarkable. It shows how stories have the power to overcome difference; they capture our imagination, and we retell the stories as we hear them, introducing into them the world that we conceive. And it is right and proper to do so. For by definition the storyteller means to turn the particular into the exemplary, and each of us supplies the details for the example. Not only so, but for the purposes of religious encounter, stories prove uniquely suited, leaving space in the telling for the hearer and reader to join in. Rabbis in the age in which Christianity was taking shape, and the Catholic storyteller many centuries later, turn out to affirm a common truth, one that, given their diversity, lays claim to self-evidence for the Western civilization that is built upon the Bible, for Christianity, and the Torah, for Judaism.

The three partners in this project extend their thanks to Richard Brown, Director of Westminster John Knox Press, who encouraged the work and brought it to fruition.

Andrew M. Greeley
Jacob Neusner
Mary Greeley Durkin

Introduction

Theological Dialogue through Trading Tales

MARY GREELEY DURKIN

The opening lines of the book of Genesis and of the Gospel of John, examples of the once-upon-a-time stories of the faith traditions of Judaism and Christianity, alert us to the intentions of our early religious storytellers. What they are about is serious business, so serious that they want us to know that their stories' roots go all the way back to the beginning. They are about to reveal to us, the hearers and readers, the story about the origins of all life and its meaning for them, their communities, and the world in which they live.

In the beginning, when God created the universe . . .

(GENESIS 1:1)

In the beginning the Word already existed; the Word was with God . . .

(JOHN 1:1)

In this respect these religious stories are not unlike every story. Stories, be they the great epics of civilization, the myths and folklore of a tradition or a nation, the legends of a specific ethnic group, children's fairy tales, family yarns, or our accounts of our day's activities, all attempt to express the significance of the experiences being recounted. Stories help us create meaning in a world that often seems bereft of meaning. Stories also are our way of sharing that meaning with others.

The rabbi and the priest are wise to turn to storytelling in their efforts to find a common ground. Theological reflection and theological dialogue are rooted in the common human experience of storytelling. Sharing stories opens us to an appreciation of our own and other cultures. Theologians, religious leaders, preachers, and religious educators ignore this at great risk.

The value of storytelling for cultural dialogue was brought home forcibly to me in my work with the National Center for Urban Ethnic Affairs in the late 1970s. As Americans became more conscious of their ethnic heritage, of their roots, the myth of the American melting pot lost its force in American society.

Sharing of stories became a way to understand how the image of a stew is a more appropriate metaphor. As individuals of Italian, Irish, Mexican, Polish, German, African American heritage told stories of their family and community life, we learned that we shared the same hopes and dreams for our families, our communities, and our country.

Stories are the poetry of our community life. While our different ethnic backgrounds often influenced our behavior, our storytelling helped us learn that we could work together for a common goal. We came to a better appreciation of the contributions the various immigrant groups, including the new immigrants, made and continue to make to our society.

A brief overview of the process of story in human experience helps us understand the importance of story for theological dialogue.

First, something happens

Many things happen during the course of a day, a week, a year, a lifetime. We share these experiences through story. Some stories make us laugh, others make us cry; some inspire hope, others fear. Certain events have great significance for us, either individually or as a community. Generally these are the experiences that speak to the questions that are common to all humans: How did life begin? What sustains us and the universe we inhabit? What happens to us when we die? Why is there good and evil?

The experience at Sinai and the experience of Easter are the central events of the communities of Judaism and Christianity. What happened to those present at these two key religious moments caused them to interpret everything, from beginning time to end time, in light of those moments. All questions of meaning are answered through the prism of the God encountered in those experiences. Correct behavior for individuals and communities follows from an understanding of the God/human relationship revealed in those events. Though the stories of Sinai and Easter are not the opening stories in either of the scriptures, they are the central stories that validate all the other stories and directives in both scriptures and in the lives of the members of the respective religious communities.

Later there is reflection on the story

Though the story itself contains the roots of its meaning, stories are subject to various interpretations, often depending on the experiences of the hearers. Traditional theology engages in this reflection as an attempt to understand the faith of the religious community. Generally, theological reflection has been a rational, most often philosophical, attempt to understand what the story says about the meaning of life for the members of the faith community. The rational understanding apart from the story speaks to us in a limited manner.

The opening line of a good story, a classic story, invites us to suspend our rationalistic, scientific mindset and enter the world of the storyteller, where we often discover a new and richer way of understanding. New images emerge out of the meeting of the story and our experiences. Questions of meaning not considered before we heard the story surface and lead us back to the story in search of a deeper level of meaning.

Classic stories are revisited again and again by individuals and communities as new experiences challenge us to search for meaning. New stories emerge from this reflection and the process repeats itself.

The stories of the oral Torah and of the Christian scriptures are classic stories that speak to the deep longings of the human heart. The rabbi and the priest turn to the stories of their respective traditions to begin a dialogue about how modern-day Christians and Jews might together renew our contemporary world.

Challenged to speak of what their faith says about the cardinal sins and cardinal virtues, they each call upon their scriptures to address these experiences. The rabbi's use of the oral Torah and the priest's use of Gospel stories and homiletic reflections are a new and innovative approach to faith dialogue. The various scripture stories chosen by the rabbi and the priest are among those that for generations have renewed, instructed, and challenged people of faith as they strive to lead lives of meaning, lives that reflect what they believe.

The role of storyteller comes naturally to the rabbi and to the priest. The rabbi's ongoing study and interpretation of the oral Torah with its wealth of stories gives him a solid base from which to enter this dialogue.

The priest, through his sociological research, came to the conclusion that the religious imagination is the most powerful indicator of how people experience God in their lives. This insight led him to write stories of God's love and eventually to use stories as homilies after the Sunday Gospel readings. His stories in this dialogue are from the homily page on his Internet home page. Each month he adds four (or five depending on the number of Sundays) new stories.[2]

The storytellers invite us to listen to their tales and enter into their dialogue. Their stories entice to us to consider how we might triumph over the evils (vices) of our society. Stories

---

2. The theologian (Mary Greeley Durkin) contributes one story to the Internet home page each month. In choosing the selections for this dialogue, the priest included one written by the theologian, unaware that it was not his own. He wonders if the reader will know which one it is.

told out of our faith perspective provide inspiring examples of how the virtues that both traditions encourage help us lead meaningful lives, lives grounded in the God of our traditions.

Theological dialogue is enhanced as we discover and reveal God through our storytelling. Elie Wiesel once said that "God made man because he loved stories." Created, as we are, in the divine image and likeness, we might add, "Humans love stories, because our God is a storyteller."

PART I

The Seven Vices

Pride

CHAPTER 1

♖ Judaic Stories

T he generation of the Flood acted arrogantly before the Omnipresent only on account of the good which he lavished on them, since it is said: Their houses are safe from fear, neither is the rod of God upon them. Their bull genders and fails not, their cow calves and casts not her calf. They send forth their little ones like a pock, and their children dance. They spend their days in prosperity and their years in pleasures.

Samson rebelled by using his eyes, as it is said: Then Samson said to his father, I saw one of the daughters of the Philistines at Timnah; now get her for me as my wife.

So he was smitten through his eyes, as it is said: And the Philistines seized him and put out his eyes.

Rabbi [Judah the Patriarch] says, "The beginning of his corruption took place in Gaza, so his punishment took place only in Gaza."

∽

Absalom rebelled through his hair, as it is said: Now in all Israel there was no one so much to be praised for his beauty as Absalom; from the sole of his foot to the crown of his head there was no blemish in him. And when he cut the hair of his head (for at the end of every year he used to cut it, when it was heavy on him, he cut it), he weighed the hair of his head, two hundred shekels by the king's weight.

Therefore he was smitten through his hair.

R. Judah the Patriarch says, "Absalom was a lifelong Nazir, and he cut his hair once in twelve months, as it is said: And at the end of four years Absalom said to the king, 'Pray let me go and pay my vow, which I have vowed to the Lord, in Hebron. For your servant vowed a vow while I dwelt at Geshur in Aram, saying, If the Lord will indeed bring me back to Jerusalem, then I will offer worship to the Lord.'"

R. Yosé says, "He cut it every Friday, for so it is the custom of kings, to cut their hair every Friday, as it is said with regard to priests: They shall not shave their heads or let their locks grow long, they shall only trim the hair of their heads."

He weighed the hair of his head, two hundred shekels by the king's weight—which the men of Tiberias and the men of Sepphoris do not do, cutting their hair on Fridays.

Because he had sexual relations with ten concubines of his father, therefore they thrust ten spearheads into his body, as it is said: And ten young men that carried Joab's armor surrounded and smote Absalom and killed him.

And since he stole three hearts—the heart of his father, and the heart of the court, and the heart of all Israel—therefore three darts were thrust into him, since it is said: And he took three darts in his hand and thrust them through the heart of Absalom.

∽

Sennacherib took pride before the Omnipresent only through an agent, as it is said: By your messengers you have mocked the Lord and you have said, "With my many chariots I have gone up the heights of the mountains. . . . I dug wells and drank foreign waters, and I dried up with the sole of my foot all the streams of Egypt."

So the Omnipresent, blessed be he, exacted punishment from him only through an agent, as it is said: And that night the messenger of the Lord went forth and slew a hundred and eighty-five thousand in the camp of the Assyrians.

And all of them were kings, with their crowns bound to their heads. Nebuchadnezzar said, "The denizens of this earth are not worthy for me to dwell among them. I shall make for myself a little cloud and dwell in it," as it is said: "I will ascend above the heights of the clouds, I will make myself like the Most High."

Said to him the Omnipresent, blessed be he: You said in your heart, I will ascend to heaven, above the stars of God I will set my throne on high—I shall bring you down to the depths of the pit.

What does it say? But you are brought down to Sheol, to the depths of the pit.

Were you the one who said, "The denizens of this earth are not worthy for me to dwell among them"?

The king said: Is not this great Babylon, which I have built by my mighty power as a royal residence and for the glory of my majesty? While the words were still in the king's mouth, there fell a voice from heaven: O King Nebuchadnezzar, to you it is spoken: The kingdom has departed from you, and you shall be driven from among men, and your dwelling shall be with the beasts of the field, and you shall be made to eat grass like an ox. All this came upon King Nebuchadnezzar at the end of twelve months.

I know only with regard to the measure of retribution that by that same measure by which a man metes out, they mete out to him. How do I know that the same is so with the measure of goodness?

Thus do you say: The measure of goodness is five hundred times greater than the measure of retribution. With regard to the measure of retribution it is written, "Visiting the sin of the fathers on the sons and on the grandsons to the third and fourth generation."

And with regard to the measure of goodness it is written, "And doing mercy for thousands." You must therefore conclude that the measure of goodness is five hundred times greater than the measure of retribution. And so you find in the case of Abraham that by that same measure by which a man metes out, they mete out to him.

He ran before the ministering angels three times, as it is said: "When he saw them, he ran to meet them," "And Abraham hastened to the tent," "And Abraham ran to the herd."

So did the Omnipresent, blessed be he, run before his children three times, as it is said: The Lord came from Sinai, and dawned from Seir upon us; he shone forth from Mount Paran.

Tosefta Sotah 3:6–17

JACOB NEUSNER COMMENTS

The sages of Judaism tell their stories in part by retelling the stories of scripture, drawing conclusions from those stories and placing them in a contemporary context. This they do by adding details, imposing points of emphasis, or otherwise reshaping the stories to make the point they wish to register. In treating the sin of pride, for example, they do not simply castigate the proud but demonstrate the idiocy of pride. This they do by taking note of the experiences of others. Those experiences show that God exacts punishment through the very matter in which people take pride: with that in which the nations of the world take pride before him, he exacts punishment from them. That pattern of human history under God's rule is now illustrated by appeal to scripture. The account of penalties for pride shades over into an account of how God's justice works, measure for measure: people are treated as they treat others. So the account of how pride is penalized now joins into a larger picture of how God metes out justice.

✠ *A Gospel Story*

Jesus also told this parable to people who were sure of their own goodness and despised everybody else. "Once there were two men who went up to the Temple to pray: one was a Pharisee, the other a tax collector. The Pharisee stood apart by himself and prayed, 'I thank you, God, that I am not greedy, dishonest, or an adulterer, like everybody else. I thank you that I am not like that tax collector over there. I fast two days a week, and I give you one tenth of all my income.' But the tax collector stood at a distance and would not even raise his face to heaven, but beat on his breast and said, 'God, have pity on me, a sinner!' I tell you," said Jesus, "the tax collector, and not the Pharisee, was in the right with God when he went home. For those who make themselves great will be humbled, and those who humble themselves will be made great."

Luke 18:9–14

ANDREW GREELEY COMMENTS

The flash of light in this parable is evident. It must have infuriated those who heard it for the first time. How dare Jesus compare a publican, a Roman tax collector, a traitor, a notorious sinner, to a man who kept all the tenets of the Jewish law and who was in every respect an upright and moral believer? Moreover, how could Jesus possibly say that the sinner was more pleasing to God than the man who kept all the rules? François Mauriac, the French Catholic novelist, once said that today one of the men would pray, Thank God I'm a good and respectable Catholic who contributes generously to the church, goes to Mass every week, and is a good friend of the parish priest. Thank God that I know I'm a humble sinner and am willing to confess my sins whenever I go to confession and not like those media celebrities who are such terrible sinners. Thank God I am a publican and not a Pharisee. Thus, Mauriac says, prays the Pharisee of today.

✠ *A Christian Story*

Once upon a time two men came to Mass, one a Catholic liberal, the other a Catholic conservative.

"Thank God," said the liberal, "that I am not a racist like this conservative; thank God that I always use politically correct language and not, as he says, 'lady' instead of 'woman'; thank God I am not a male chauvinist, like he is; thank God I support all the good liberal causes, I'm pro-environment, I recycle everything I can, and I defend whales and snail darters and all other endangered species. I'm glad I'm not a hypocrite like he is who pretends to be a good Catholic and hates immigrants. We shouldn't permit phonies like him in the church."

And the conservative said, "Thank God that I agree with everything the Holy Father says, that I'm pro-life and against birth control, and think that divorce should not be permitted and kids should be forced into line, and that it is time to end our permissiveness toward those who will not work or those who threaten our family values or those who are destroying our country by coming to it illegally and those who do not have a solid work ethic like I do. Thank God I am a strict, God-fearing Catholic and not a cafeteria Catholic like he is."

Someone asked St. Brigid which of them was the better human being. "Would you want to live with either of them?" she asked. "Haven't they missed something altogether? Does either one ever question his certainties? Does either of them try to love even those who are closest to him? Sure, isn't your crop of Pharisees as large now as it ever was?"

✙ *A Gospel Story*

"You are like salt for the whole human race. But if salt loses its saltiness, there is no way to make it salty again. It has become worthless, so it is thrown out and people trample on it. You are like light for the whole world. A city built on a hill cannot be hid. No one lights a lamp and puts it under a bowl; instead it is put on the lampstand, where it gives light for everyone in the house. In the same way your light must shine before people, so that they will see the good things you do and praise your Father in heaven."

Matthew 5:13–16

ANDREW GREELEY COMMENTS

The Sermon on the Mount in the book of Matthew was a sermon that was never given. Rather it is a construct, a literary device that the evangelist uses to pull together in one place teachings of Jesus which appear in different places in the earlier traditions. It is a summary of much of what Jesus said and taught (as this was remembered in later years), a compendium of his wisdom. Moreover the compendium is designed specifically for the instruction, not of the crowds to whom Jesus preached in Galilee, but of the early Christian community. In this passage Jesus, as edited by the evangelist, is warning the early Christians that he and his good news will be judged by their behavior. It is well for Christians today to reflect on that truth. If Christianity has a terrible image with many people, it is in substantial part the fault of Christians.

✠ *A Christian Story*

Once upon a time Molly Whupi and the girls' basketball team from Mother Mary High School went all the way across town to play a *public* school that they had never played before. It was a tough game, much tougher than Molly and her team expected. From the very beginning there were fights with the other players, the other coaches, the refs, and the crowd. Mother Mary's team, I blush to admit, talked a lot of trash, committed unnecessary fouls, and had four technicals called against it. Their coach and two of their players were ejected from the game. The rest of the team screamed at the crowd like a bunch of fifth-graders, tough fifth-graders—though fifth-graders wouldn't know such bad language (well, actually they would, but they'd be less likely to use it in public). Finally, the Mother Mary girls won, but they stomped off the court without saying anything nice to the players on the host team. Later, one of the nuns said, "Well, I hope those poor people don't judge all Catholic school students by the way you people acted. Totally gross. Like you were totally not the salt of the earth or the light of the world." Molly knew the Sister was right, so she persuaded the other girls to send letters of apology to the principal and the coach and the captain of the other team.

Covetousness

CHAPTER 2

A Judaic Story

Alexander of Macedonia went to the king of Kasia, beyond the mountains of darkness. He came to a certain town, called Cartagena, and it was populated entirely by women.

They came out before him and said to him, "If you make war on us and conquer us, word will spread about you that you destroyed a town of women. But if we do battle with you and conquer you, word will spread about you that you made war on women and they beat you. And you'll never again be able to hold up your head among kings."

At that moment he turned away and left. After he went away, he wrote on the door of the gate of the city, saying, "I, Alexander the Macedonian, a king, was a fool until I came to the town called Cartagena, and I learned wisdom from women."

He came to another town, called Africa. They came out and greeted him with apples made out of gold, golden pomegranates, and golden bread.

He said, "Is this gold what you eat in your country?"

They said to him, "And is it not this way in your country, that you have come here?"

He said to them, "It is not your wealth that I have come to see, but it is your justice that I have come to see."

While they were standing there, two men came before the king for justice.

This one kept himself far from thievery, and so did that. One of them said, "I bought a rubbish heap from this man. I dug it open and found a jewel in it. I said to him, 'Take your jewel. I bought a rubbish heap. A jewel I didn't buy.'"

The other said, "When I sold the rubbish heap to that man, I sold him the rubbish heap and everything that is in it."

The king called one of them and said to him, "Do you have a male child?"

He said to him, "Yes."

The king called the other and said to him, "Do you have a daughter?"

He said to him, "Yes."

Then the king said to them, "Let this one marry that one, and let the two of them enjoy the jewel." Alexander of Macedonia began to express surprise.

He said to him, "Why are you surprised? Did I not give a good judgment?"

He said to him, "Yes, you did."

He said to him, "If this case had come to court in your country, how would you have judged it?"

He said to him, "We should have cut off the head of this party and cut off the head of that party, and the jewel would have passed into the possession of the crown."

He said to him, "Does rain fall on you?"

He said to him, "Yes."

"And does the sun rise for you?"

He said to him, "Yes."

He said to him, "Are there small cattle in your country?"

He said to him, "Yes."

"Woe to you! It is on account of the merit of the small cattle that you are saved."

That is in line with the following verse of Scripture: Man and beast you save, O Lord. "Man on account of the merit of the beast do you save, O Lord."

Pesiqta de Rab Kahana IX.I.8

JACOB NEUSNER COMMENTS

"Thou shalt not covet" is one of the two of the Ten Commandments that made it onto the list of the seven deadly sins. The other is lust ("thou shalt not commit adultery")—and lust comes about through coveting another's mate. People naturally are competitive, but for many, competition spills over into contention. For if the other accomplishes something more, the one feels diminished. In this remarkable story sages portray the just and the unjust government. The unjust government covets the property of its subjects. The story here shows how the greatest king of all time, Alexander, coveted other peoples' wealth but learned wisdom in a remote, obscure place, and from the women of that place.

A Judaic Story

From the following story that R. Haninah tells:

Some old rabbis bought a pile of wheat from some soldiers, and found in it a pouch filled with money, and they returned it to them. The soldiers said, "Blessed be the God of the Jews."

Abba Oshaiah was a laundryman in a bathhouse. The queen came to wash there and lost her jewels and gold pieces. He found them and returned them to her.

She said, "They are yours for you have acquired possession of them. As to me, what are these worth to me? I have many which are even better than these."

He said to her, "The Torah has decreed that we should return what we find."

She said, "Blessed be the God of the Jews."

R. Samuel bar Suseretai went to Rome. The queen had lost her jewelry. He found it. A proclamation went forth through the city: "Whoever returns her jewelry in thirty days will receive thus and so. If he returns it after thirty days, his head will be cut off." He did not return the jewelry within thirty days. After thirty days, he returned it to her.

She said to him, "Weren't you in town?"

He said to her, "Yes, I was here."

She said to him, "And didn't you hear the proclamation?"

He said to her, "Yes, I heard it."

She said to him, "And what did it say?"

He said to her that it said, 'Whoever returns the jewelry in thirty days will receive thus-and-so. If he returns it after thirty days, his head will be cut off."

She said to him, "And why didn't you return it within thirty days?"

"So that people should not say, 'It was because I was afraid of you that I did so.' But it was because I fear the All-Merciful."

She said to him. "Blessed be the God of the Jews."

Yerushalmi Baba Mesia 1:5

Jacob Neusner comments

The virtuous man does not covet the property of others and will not accept what does not belong to him. Here an exemplary sage does not covet the property of a Saracen, even though by strict law, if not in true justice, he has the right to keep that property. Here we see the opposite of covetousness, which is honesty beyond the measure of the law.

✠ *A Gospel Story*

"If your brother sins against you, go to him and show him his fault. But do it privately, just between yourselves. If he listens to you, you have won your brother back. But if he will not listen to you, take one or two other persons with you, so that 'every accusation may be upheld by the testimony of two or more witnesses,' as the scripture says. And if he will not listen to them, then tell the whole thing to the church. Finally, if he will not listen to the church, treat him as though he were a pagan or a tax collector.

"And so I tell all of you: what you prohibit on earth will be prohibited in heaven, and what you permit on earth will be permitted in heaven.

"And I tell you more: whenever two of you on earth agree about anything you pray for, it will be done for you by my Father in heaven. For where two or three come together in my name, I am there with them."

Matthew 18:15–20

ANDREW GREELEY COMMENTS

This instruction was meant for the early church, which was split by many internal conflicts. There was not, as one recent author said, a single church but many churches that were part of a movement. Within congregations and among congregations there was constant controversy (so nothing much has changed). The author is trying to use the instructions of Jesus about love as a kind of rule of thumb for settling controversies and conflicts. It is strange, is it not, that Jesus' message of love was forgotten so soon after his own time, and that Cardinal Bernardin's recent attempt to persuade warring Catholic factions not to fight one another is merely a continuation of what St. Matthew is trying to do in the Gospel.

✠ *A Christian Story*

Once upon a time there was a poker club, four men who gathered on the first Tuesday of each month to play penny ante. Not much money ever changed hands, and all had a good time. One man brought the cards, another brought chips, a third brought beer, and a fourth brought popcorn. The wife of whoever was the host made sandwiches and then, with a sigh of relief, joined the other three wives at a movie. One night a wife tried to be a little fancy and made hamburgers. The next time the wife made pasta, the time after that there was Caesar salad, the fourth time there were steaks. I must not accuse the wives of starting the competition because they were doing only what their husbands asked. Then the man whose turn it was to bring the beer brought Guinness stout, and the beer competition began. Someone suggested that they ought to play for a dime a point. Pretty soon the poker club was split by rivalry and competition. Everyone tried to outdo everyone else. There was a fight at almost every session. The four men began to dislike and then hate one another. The poker club collapsed. None of the men ever played poker again.

✠ A Gospel Story

In Samaria he came to a town named Sychar, which was not far from the field that Jacob had given to his son Joseph. Jacob's well was there, and Jesus, tired out by the trip, sat down by the well. It was about noon.

A Samaritan woman came to draw some water, and Jesus said to her, "Give me a drink of water." (His disciples had gone into town to buy food.)

The woman answered, "You are a Jew, and I am a Samaritan—so how can you ask me for a drink?" (Jews will not use the same cups and bowls that Samaritans use.)

Jesus answered, "If you only knew what God gives and who it is that is asking you for a drink, you would ask him, and he would give you life-giving water."

"Sir," the woman said, "you don't have a bucket, and the well is deep. Where would you get that life-giving water? It was our ancestor Jacob who gave us this well; he and his children and his flocks all drank from it. You don't claim to be greater than Jacob, do you?"

Jesus answered, "Those who drink this water will get thirsty again, but those who drink the water that I will give them will never be thirsty again. The water that I will give them will become in them a spring which will provide them with life-giving water and give them eternal life."

"Sir," the woman said, "give me that water! Then I will never be thirsty again, nor will I have to come here to draw water."

"Go and call your husband," Jesus told her, "and come back."

"I don't have a husband," she answered.

Jesus replied, "You are right when you say you don't have a husband. You have been married to five men, and the man you live with now is not really your husband. You have told me the truth."

"I see you are a prophet, sir," the woman said. "My Samaritan ancestors worshiped God on this mountain, but you Jews say that Jerusalem is the place where we should worship God."

Jesus said to her, "Believe me, woman, the time will come when people will not worship the Father either on this mountain or in Jerusalem. You Samaritans do not really know whom you worship; but we Jews know whom we worship, because it is from the Jews that salvation comes. But the time is coming and is already here, when by the power of God's Spirit people will worship the Father as he really is, offering him the true worship that he wants. God is Spirit, and only by the power of his Spirit can people worship him as he really is."

The woman said to him, "I know that the Messiah will come, and when he comes, he will tell us everything."

Jesus answered, "I am he, I who am talking with you."

At that moment Jesus' disciples returned, and they were greatly surprised to find him talking with a woman. But none of them said to her, "What do you want?" or asked him, "Why are you talking with her?"

Then the woman left her water jar, went back to the town, and said to the people there, "Come and see the man who told me everything I have ever done. Could he be the Messiah?" So they left the town and went to Jesus.

In the meantime the disciples were begging Jesus, "Teacher, have something to eat!"

But he answered, "I have food to eat that you know nothing about."

So the disciples started asking among themselves, "Could somebody have brought him food?"

"My food," Jesus said to them, "is to obey the will of the one who sent me and to finish the work he gave me to do. You have a saying, 'Four more months and then the harvest.' But I tell you, take a good look at the fields; the crops are now ripe and ready to be harvested! The one who reaps the harvest is being paid and gathers the crops for eternal life; so the one who plants and the one who reaps will be glad together. For the saying is true, 'Someone plants, someone else reaps.' I have sent you to reap a harvest in a field where you did not work; others worked there, and you profit from their work."

Many of the Samaritans in that town believed in Jesus because the woman had said, "He told me everything I have ever done." So when the Samaritans came to him, they begged him to stay with them, and Jesus stayed there two days.

Many more believed because of his message, and they told the woman, "We believe now, not because of what you said, but because we ourselves have heard him, and we know that he really is the Savior of the world."

John 4:5–42

ANDREW GREELEY COMMENTS

There is no reason to think that this story does not refer to an event that happened during the life of Jesus, especially since a conversation between him and a Samaritan woman would have been a bit shocking in the early church. However, in its present form it is a theological reflection in dramatic form; indeed, one written by a very skilled dramatist. It is not impossible that in fact this was a one-act liturgical play acted out by early Christians as part of the baptismal ritual. The Sufi mystic Rumi once wrote apropos of God and humans, "Thirst seeks water, but water seeks thirst." That would be a good summary of this Gospel story. Certainly Jesus defies all the politically correct conventions of his time by talking to such a person, thus denouncing implicitly all ethnic and gender prejudices.

Certainly also it is a love story, harking back to the love stories at the well of Isaac and Jacob. But above all it is a story about thirst, about St. Augustine's "You have made us for yourself alone, O Lord, and our hearts are restless till they rest in you."

✠ *A Christian Story*

Once upon a time there was a man who was a prisoner of war. The camp in which he was held was a cruel, harsh place and the guards were brutal. Many men died. Our soldier was sick often and hungry always. Once he almost died of thirst. But his worst suffering was the separation from his home and family and his fear that he would never see them again. Every day he prayed that he might live long enough to go home and quench his thirst for his family. Finally after many years the war was over and he went home. He was deliriously happy to be reunited with his wife and children and they with him. But as time went on it seemed to him that they didn't understand all that he had suffered and the terrible thirst he had experienced for their love. "You don't understand," he said often, "you just don't understand what it was like." Finally his teenage daughter said to him, "Daddy, you don't understand what it was like for us."

Lust

CHAPTER 3

▼ A Judaic Story

When a man arouses himself and goes to commit fornication, all of his limbs obey him, because the impulse to do evil is king over the two hundred and forty-eight limbs. But when he goes to carry out a religious duty, all his limbs begin to drag, because the impulse to do evil from the womb is king over the two hundred and forty-eight limbs that are in a man.

The impulse to do good is only like one who is imprisoned, as it is said: For out of prison he came forth to be king, referring to the impulse to do good.

Now there are those who say that this verse refers to Joseph, the righteous man. When that wicked woman Potiphar's wife came, she disturbed him by her words, saying to him, "I shall lock you up in prison if you do not go to bed with me."

He said to her, "The Lord loosens prisoners."

She said to him, "I shall put out your eyes."

He said to her, "The Lord opens the eyes of the blind."

She said to him, "I shall force you to stoop."

He said to her, "The Lord raises up those who are bowed down."

She said to him, "I shall make you wicked."

He said to her, "The Lord loves the righteous."

She said to him, "I shall make you into an Aramaean."
He said to her, "The Lord preserves strangers."
Finally he said, "How shall I commit this great evil?"

The Fathers according to R. Nathan XVI:III–V

JACOB NEUSNER COMMENTS

Among the variety of acts of rebellion against God, sexual immorality finds the highest place on the list. In presenting teachings and stories about lust, sages underscored the resources that we have to overcome it. Their presentation is analytical, not merely narrative, but the analysis sets the stage for the stories of how great saints and sages overcame this deadly sin.

A Judaic Story

There is the case of a man who was meticulous about carrying out the religious duty of the fringes. He heard that there was a certain whore, in one of the coastal towns, who would collect a fee of four hundred gold coins. He sent her four hundred gold coins and made a date with her.

When his time came, he came along and took a seat at the door of her house. Her maid came and told her, "That man with whom you made a date, lo, he is sitting at the door of the house."

She said to her, "Let him come in."

When he came in, she spread out for him seven silver mattresses and one gold one, and she was on the top, and between each one were silver stools, and on the top, gold ones. When he came to do the deed, the four fringes fell out of his garment and appeared to him like four witnesses. The man slapped himself in the face and immediately withdrew and took a seat on the ground.

The whore too withdrew and took a seat on the ground.

She said to him, "By the winged god of Rome! I shall not let you go until you tell me what blemish you have found in me."

He said to her, "By the Temple service! I did not find any blemish at all in you, for in the whole world there is none so beautiful as you. But the Lord, our God, has imposed upon me a rather small duty, but concerning even that minor matter he wrote, 'I am the Lord your God who brought you out of the land of Egypt to be your God. I am the Lord your God'—two times.

"I am the Lord your God,' I am destined to pay a good reward.

"I am the Lord your God,' I am destined to exact punishment."

She said to him, "By the Temple service! I shall not let you go until you write me your name, the name of your town, and the name of your school in which you study Torah."

So he wrote for her his name, the name of his town, the name of his master, and the name of the school in which he had studied Torah.

She went and split up her entire wealth, a third to the government, a third to the poor, and a third she took with her and came and stood at the schoolhouse of R. Hiyya.

She said to him, "My lord, accept me as a proselyte."

He said to her, "Is it possible that you have laid eyes on one of the disciples and are converting in order to marry him?"

She took the slip out that was in her hand.

He said to the disciple who had paid the money but not gone through with the act, "Stand up and acquire possession of what you have purchased. Those spreads that she spread out for you in violation of a prohibition she will now spread out for you in full remission of the prohibition.

"As to this one, the recompense is paid out in this world, and as to the world to come, I do not know how much more he will receive!"

Sifré to Numbers CXV

JACOB NEUSNER COMMENTS

In Judaism the remedy for lust is devotion to study and practice of the Torah, and in this case we see how a lustful man ultimately was kept from the sin of lust by reason of his observance of the commandment to wear fringes on his garments. These fringes, on a garment close to the body, reminded him of his obligations to God and prevented him from sinning. Impressed by such steadfastness in the face of temptation, the whore gave up her profession and accepted the Torah and the God who reveals it.

✠ A Gospel Story

The next day John saw Jesus coming to him, and said, "There is the Lamb of God, who takes away the sin of the world! This is the one I was talking about when I said, 'A man is coming after me, but he is greater than I am, because he existed before I was born. I did not know who he would be, but I came baptizing with water in order to make him known to the people of Israel.'"

And John gave this testimony: "I saw the Spirit come down like a dove from heaven and stay on him. I still did not know that he was the one, but God, who sent me to baptize with water, had said to me, 'You will see the Spirit come down and stay on a man; he is the one who baptizes with the Holy Spirit.' I have seen it," said John, "and I tell you that he is the Son of God."

John 1:29–34

ANDREW GREELEY COMMENTS

The baptism of Jesus was a problem for his followers. John's disciples could always lord it over the disciples of Jesus: "Our master baptized your master, nah, nah, nah!" It also creates a problem for those hyper-orthodox Catholics today who so emphasize the divinity in Jesus that there is little room for his humanity. They are also boxed in by the phrase that Jesus grew in wisdom, age, and grace. Any suggestion that God might grow scares them. An authentic Christology, however, which sees Jesus like the rest of us in all things save sin, sees no problem in his listening to the Baptist and going through a ceremony of renewal and rededication before he began his public life. Did Jesus learn anything from the Baptist? If, like all humans, he grew in understanding and maturity, the only appropriate answer is that of course he did.

✠ *A Christian Story*

Once upon a time there was a young man who was charming, handsome, witty, and a great athlete. Everyone in his school adored him, especially one quiet, thoughtful girl who was too shy to talk to him. Someone told him about her adoration. He dismissed her with a laugh. She was pretty and smart, but not good enough for him. Eventually he married someone else and lived a life of noisy desperation with her. At their twenty-fifth high school reunion, his wife had become an ugly shrew and he himself was an overweight failure, his best days long ago on a football field. The quiet girl had become a famous writer and was the most beautiful woman at the reunion. Her husband was a successful doctor who told everyone that he would not have made it through medical school without his wife's support and determination. On the way home after the party, the one-time hero thought, very briefly, that he had failed to recognize what the shy and quiet girl really was. So too we often fail to recognize Jesus in those we encounter and for the same reason—we do not take the time to look.

✠ *A Gospel Story*

On that same day two of Jesus' followers were going to a village named Emmaus, about seven miles from Jerusalem, and they were talking to each other about all the things that had happened. As they talked and discussed, Jesus himself drew near and walked along with them; they saw him, but somehow did not recognize him. Jesus said to them, "What are you talking about to each other, as you walk along?"

They stood still, with sad faces. One of them, named Cleopas, asked him, "Are you the only visitor in Jerusalem who doesn't know the things that have been happening there these last few days?"

"What things?" he asked.

"The things that happened to Jesus of Nazareth," they answered. "This man was a prophet and was considered by God and by all the people to be powerful in everything he said and did. Our chief priests and rulers handed him over to be sentenced to death, and he was crucified. And we had hoped that he would be the one who was going to set Israel free! Besides all that, this is now the third day since it happened. Some of the women of our group surprised us; they went at dawn to the tomb, but could not find his body. They came back saying they had seen a vision of angels who told them that he is alive. Some of our group went to the tomb and found it exactly as the women had said, but they did not see him."

Then Jesus said to them, "How foolish you are; how slow you are to believe everything the prophets said! Was it not necessary for the Messiah to suffer these things and then to enter his glory?" And Jesus explained to them what was said about himself in all the Scriptures, beginning with the books of Moses and the writings of all the prophets.

Luke 24:13–35

ANDREW GREELEY COMMENTS

The Easter experience of the early Christians was that a union that had been rent by death had been restored in loving communion. Jesus, who had been with them and then was with them no longer, now was with them again, indeed more closely united with them than ever before. They were especially moved that repeatedly he ate with them. What better sign of a communion of love with those whom you love and who love you than breaking bread together. Then they began to understand that when they gathered together around the table for their common meal Jesus was still with them and would always be with them. The Eucharist became a celebration of the presence of Jesus among them even when he wasn't visibly present. The trick was to see him present among the others when they broke bread together. So the story of the two disciples who were getting out of town while the getting was good became a eucharistic story, a story that said Jesus was present whenever the community of his followers broke bread together and indeed whenever people who loved one another ate a common meal.

✠ *A Christian Story*

Once upon a time a husband and a wife were having a lot of conflict with each other. They fought over money, they fought over the time they spent with their family, they fought over where they would go on their vacations, they fought over their children, and, of course, they fought over what the fights were about. Once the man and woman had been deeply in love with each other. They thought that they were still in love with each other. Only there were so many things to do in life that the conflicts had filled up the time that used to be devoted to love. They knew they weren't close to anything like divorce. Well, not yet anyway. Finally the man suggested one night that they get a baby-sitter and go out for dinner. The woman said they didn't have time for that any more, but the man insisted. (I realize that usually in such stories it is the woman who insists. But I thought I'd fight gender stereotyping in this story). Well, the meal was wonderful and they relaxed and had a good time and a great conversation, and they saw how silly their quarrels had been and how easy it would be to avoid them, especially if they went out for dinner more often.

"You know," the wife said on the way home, "it was almost as if God were with us while we were eating, guiding us to see how foolish we've been." (Again I fight gender stereotyping by giving the man's line to the woman.)

"Maybe," her husband replied, "he was. Maybe it's not just at Mass that Jesus is present among us."

Anger

CHAPTER 4

🕎 A Judaic Story

S aid R. Samuel bar Nahman:
Ulla went up to the Land of Israel, accompanied by two men from Khuzistan. One of them went and killed the other. He said to Ulla, "So didn't I do the right thing?"

He said to him, "Yessirree! And now cut his throat right across."

When he came before R. Yohanan, he said to him, "Maybe— God forbid—I have encouraged sinners?"

He said to him, "You saved your life."

R. Yohanan expressed surprise: "It is written, 'There the Lord will give them a temperamental heart'—this speaks of Babylonia—so how could such a thing have happened in the Land of Israel, where people are patient with one another?"

Ulla said to him, "At that moment we had not yet crossed the Jordan."

Mishnah Tractate Nedarim 3:1/22A–B

JACOB NEUSNER COMMENTS

As with other temporal emotions, the sages have little patience for anything that causes a loss of control over the mind. The mark of wisdom is not to give way to anger or lose one's temper. As is often the case, we find a presentation in general terms, followed by an illustrative story.

🕎 *A Judaic Story*

Our rabbis have taught on Tannaite authority:

A person always should be humble, like Hillel the Elder, and not captious, like Shammai the Elder.

There was the case of two people who made a bet with each other for four hundred zuz.

They stipulated, "Whoever can infuriate Hillel will get the four hundred zuz."

One of them went to try. That day was a Friday, toward nightfall, and Hillel was washing his hair. The man came and knocked on the door, saying, "Where is Hillel, where is Hillel?"

Hillel wrapped himself up in his cloak and came to meet him. He said to him, "My son, what do you require?"

He said to him, "I have a question to ask."

He said to him, "Ask, my son, ask."

He said to him, "How come the Babylonians have round heads?"

He said to him, "My son, you have asked quite a question: It's because they don't have skilled midwives."

He went and waited a while and came back and knocked on the door. He said, "Who's here? Who's here?"

Hillel wrapped himself up in his cloak and came out.

He said to him, "My son, what do you need?"

He said to him, "Why are the eyes of the people of Palmyra Tadmor bleary?"

He said to him, "My son, you've asked quite a question. It's because they live in the sands of the desert and the winds blow and scatter the sand in their eyes. Therefore their eyes are bleary."

He went and waited a while and came back and knocked on the door. He said, "Who's here? Who's here?"

Hillel wrapped himself up in his cloak and came out.

He said to him, "My son, what do you need?"

He said to him, "I need to ask a question."

He said to him, "Go ahead."

He said to him, "Why are the feet of the Africans flat?"

He said to him, "Because they live by swamps, and every day walk in water, therefore their feet are flat."

He said to him, "I have a lot of questions to ask, but I'm afraid that you'll get mad."

He said to him, "Whatever questions you have, go and ask."

He said to him, "Are you the Hillel, whom people call the patriarch of Israel?"

He said to him, "Yup."

He said to him, "Well, if that's who you are, then I hope there won't be many in Israel like you!"

He said to him, "My son, how come?"

He said to him, "You have cost me four hundred zuz."

He said to him, "You should be careful of your moods! Hillel is worth your losing four hundred zuz without Hillel's losing his temper."

Bavli to Mishnah Tractate Shabbat 2:5/30B–31A

JACOB NEUSNER COMMENTS

The sage Hillel serves as the model of one who held his temper even when provoked, in contrast to his rival, Shammai, who lost his temper easily and gave way to anger.

✠ *A Gospel Story*

From that time on Jesus began to say plainly to his disciples, "I must go to Jerusalem and suffer much from the elders, the chief priests, and the teachers of the Law. I will be put to death, but three days later I will be raised to life."

Peter took him aside and began to rebuke him. "God forbid it, Lord!" he said. "That must never happen to you!"

Jesus turned around and said to Peter, "Get away from me, Satan! You are an obstacle in my way, because these thoughts of yours don't come from God, but from human nature."

Then Jesus said to his disciples, "If any of you want to come with me, you must forget yourself, carry your cross, and follow me. For if you want to save your own life, you will lose it; but if you lose your life for my sake, you will find it. Will you gain anything if you win the whole world but lose your life? Of course not! There is nothing you can give to regain your life. For the Son of Man is about to come in the glory of his Father with his angels, and then he will reward each one according to his deeds. I assure you that there are some here who will not die until they have seen the Son of Man come as King."

Matthew 16:21–28

ANDREW GREELEY COMMENTS

We must read the Gospel stories with an awareness that the authors are aiming their messages at the problems of the Christian community to which they are writing. Many early Christians (and remember that there were probably no more than a thousand at the end of the first century) found it hard to accept the fact that their leader, a man who was the son of God in a special way, would have died the horrible and humiliating death of crucifixion, a death reserved for criminals and slaves. Peter's protest is in effect their protest. Life must be lost, Jesus responds. All of us must die, therefore he had to die too, since he was one of us. He showed us how to die and brought God down with us into the valley of death.

✠ A Christian Story

Once upon a time there was a little boy whose dog was killed by a car when the dog ran across the street. The boy was furious at the teenager who drove the car. He shouted at him and hit him.

"I didn't mean to do it," said the teen.

"But you did it," said the boy, "and I hate you." It was the first time the boy had ever seen anything that was dead, and this was a dog that was very dear to him.

The boy's mother tried to explain to him that everything living must die. "If you live, then you will die. Someday Daddy and I will die just like your grandparents you never knew. Someday you will die too. But we believe that love is as strong as death, so nothing that God loves ever really dies."

The little boy thought about it for a while and then asked whether God loved his dog. The mommy said that she was sure God did. "So then doggy really isn't dead."

The mommy reached for an answer: "Everything that is in the mind of God exists forever," she said.

The little boy brightened. "Then," he said, "everything will be all right."

"Yes," said the mommy, "everything will be all right and all manner of things will be all right."

✠ *A Gospel Story*

Then Peter came to Jesus and asked, "Lord, if my brother keeps on sinning against me, how many times do I have to forgive him? Seven times?"

"No, not seven times," answered Jesus, "but seventy times seven, because the Kingdom of heaven is like this. Once there was a king who decided to check on his servants' accounts. He had just begun to do so when one of them was brought in who owed him millions of dollars. The servant did not have enough to pay his debt, so the king ordered him to be sold as a slave, with his wife and his children and all that he had, in order to pay the debt. The servant fell on his knees before the king. 'Be patient with me,' he begged, 'and I will pay you everything!' The king felt sorry for him, so he forgave him the debt and let him go.

"Then the man went out and met one of his fellow servants who owed him a few dollars. He grabbed him and started choking him. 'Pay back what you owe me!' he said. His fellow servant fell down and begged him, 'Be patient with me, and I will pay you back!' But he refused; instead, he had him thrown into jail until he should pay the debt. When the other servants saw what had happened, they were very upset and went to the king and told him everything. So he called the servant in. 'You worthless slave!' he said. 'I forgave you the whole amount you owed me, just because you asked me to. You should have had mercy on your fellow servant, just as I had mercy on you.' The king was very angry, and he sent the servant to jail to be punished until he should pay back the whole amount."

And Jesus concluded, "That is how my Father in heaven will treat every one of you unless you forgive your brother from your heart."

Matthew 18:21–35

ANDREW GREELEY COMMENTS

This story instructs the conflict-ridden members of the early Christian community. It recalls an incident recounted in the tradition (which may have had many more Jesus/Peter stories than are available to us today) in which Peter again plays the straight man for Jesus. The Lord has told them that God is forgiving love—the essence of the revelation of Jesus and of the Christian message. So if God is forgiving love, we must forgive too, right? All right, says Peter, setting Jesus up, how many times? Seven? Poor Peter lost again. Just as there are no limits to God's forgiveness, so there must be no limits to our forgiveness. One has to say that this theme has not always been honored in the Christian community.

✠ A Christian Story

A brother and sister fought all the time, from the first moment the little girl discovered that her monopoly on her parents had been broken by the arrival of the new little monster. She picked on him and found fault with everything he did from day one. As soon as he learned that there was a rival in the family who did not like him, he began fighting back. They heckled each other, made fun of each other, tattled on each other, criticized each other, ridiculed each other. Nothing their parents could do would stop the fighting. When they were teens they bickered all the time, made fun of each other's friends, and reported each other to their parents. One day at a party the sister made so much fun of her brother's date that the brother said to her, "I wish you were dead." The sister was in an auto accident on the way home and was killed. The boy never got over it. All his life he mourned for his sister and blamed himself for her death. "Why couldn't we stop fighting?" he often said. Maybe in purgatory they'll finally make up.

Envy

CHAPTER 5

🕎 *A Judaic Story*

A sage takes precedence over a king; a king takes precedence over a high priest; a high priest takes precedence over a prophet; a prophet takes precedence over a priest anointed for war; a priest anointed for war takes precedence over the head of a priestly watch; the head of a priestly watch takes precedence over the head of a household of priests; the head of a household of priests takes precedence over the superintendent of the cashiers; the superintendent of the cashiers takes precedence over the Temple treasurer; the Temple treasurer takes precedence over an ordinary priest; an ordinary priest takes precedence over a Levite; a Levite takes precedence over an Israelite; an Israelite takes precedence over a *mamzer*, the offspring of a union of a man and a woman who are not legally permitted to marry; a *mamzer* takes precedence over a Netin, the offspring of the caste of Temple servants; a Netin takes precedence over a proselyte; a proselyte takes precedence over a freed slave.

Under what circumstances? When all of them are equivalent.

But if the *mamzer* is a disciple of a sage, and a high priest is an ignoramus, the *mamzer* who is the disciple of a sage takes precedence over a high priest who is an ignoramus.

A sage takes precedence over a king.
For if a sage dies, we have none who is like him.
If a king dies, any Israelite is suitable to mount the
throne.

Tosefta Horayot 2:8

JACOB NEUSNER COMMENTS

Envy fuels hatred, contempt, fear, and loathing; it is the single most common emotion. Whether among siblings or in clubs or in businesses, offices, and professions, no single emotion brings more malice or ill will than sheer loathing of someone who has more, or does more, than the norm. Envy is the price of excellence, and the one who is envied, whether proud or humble, cannot do much about it.

A Judaic Story

It has been taught on Tannaite authority: R. Meir says, "The omnipresent has varied a man in three ways: appearance, intelligence, and voice; intelligence, because of robbers and thieves, and appearance and voice, because of the possibilities of licentiousness."

Man was created on Friday, last in order of creation.

And why was man created last?

So that he should not grow proud.

For they can say to him, "The mosquito came before you in the order of the works of creation."

They have made a parable: To what is the matter comparable?

To a king who built a palace and dedicated it and prepared a meal and only afterward invited the guests.

And so Scripture says, "The wisest of women has built her house."

This refers to the King of the kings of kings, blessed be he, who built his world in seven days by wisdom.

"She has hewn out her seven pillars"—these are the seven days of creation.

"She has killed her beasts and mixed her wine"—these are the oceans, rivers, wastes, and all the other things which the world needs.

"She has sent forth her maidens, she cries on the high places of the city: Who is simple—let him turn in hither, and he who is void of understanding"—these refer to Adam and Eve.

Bavli to M Sanhedrin 4:5J/Bavli Sanhedrin 38A

JACOB NEUSNER COMMENTS

Sages deemed all persons created equally responsible before God, but different in standing and achievement. They viewed society as a hierarchy, with certain inherited, sacred tasks marking out one class of persons as higher than another. But at the same time, they insisted, the marks of status give way before the achievements of intellect, so that mastery of the Torah raises a person of low status and ignorance lowers a person of high status. In the end, therefore, status is not conferred, for instance by noble ancestry, but it is achieved by solid work in learning in the Torah.

✠ A Gospel Story

Jesus again used parables in talking to the people. "The Kingdom of heaven is like this. Once there was a king who prepared a wedding feast for his son. He sent his servants to tell the invited guests to come to the feast, but they did not want to come. So he sent other servants with this message for the guests: 'My feast is ready now, my steers and prize calves have been butchered, and everything is ready. Come to the wedding feast!' But the invited guests paid no attention and went about their business: one went to his farm, another to his store, while others grabbed the servants, beat them, and killed them. The king was very angry; so he sent his soldiers, who killed those murderers and burned down their city. Then he called his servants and said to them, 'My wedding feast is ready, but the people I invited did not deserve it. Now go to the main streets and invite to the feast as many people as you find.' So the servants went out into the streets and gathered all the people they could find, good and bad alike; and the wedding hall was filled with people.The king went in to look at the guests and saw a man who was not wearing wedding clothes. 'Friend, how did you get in here without wedding clothes?' the king asked him. But the man said nothing. Then the king told the servants, 'Tie him up hand and foot, and throw him outside in the dark. There he will cry and gnash his teeth.'"

And Jesus concluded, "Many are invited, but few are chosen."

Matthew 22:1–14

ANDREW GREELEY COMMENTS

We hear another parable of urgency, another tale of monumental stupidity, another narrative about stupid, ungrateful, self-destructive human beings. The idiocy of the characters in this story boggles the mind. How can anyone be that stupid! How can people refuse an invitation to what will be a grand party!

✠ *A Christian Story*

Once upon a time a little girl was about to have her seventh birthday party. Now all know how little girls enjoy birthday parties, especially their own. But this particular little girl—I think her name was Fiona—was really a birthday freak. She loved birthday parties more than any other girl her age in the whole parish. She wanted everyone to have fun at the party. Her parents bought videotapes and cookies and cake and ice cream and some very special prizes for everyone that came. She invited every little girl she knew to the party. They all knew how generous she was at other parties so they were certain that the party would be perfectly splendid. Some even said, "The presents she will give us at her own party will be better than the ones we will give her. It'll be fun and totally a good deal besides." But some of the little girls, the most popular ones of course, were unhappy that she had invited everyone, even the geeks. What fun would a party be if the geeks were there. So those that weren't geeks (that is, they thought they weren't, because they were the worst of the geeks) made up excuses for not coming. Then the rest said, well, no one is going to be at her party, so we won't go either. On the day of the party only four little girls showed up. What were they going to do with all the food and the games and the prizes? Well, the birthday girl saw that all the boys were hanging around outside, so she let them in. The boys were very well behaved and hardly broke anything. And they helped clean up afterward.

✠ *A Gospel Story*

"The Kingdom of heaven is like this. Once there was a man who went out early in the morning to hire some men to work in his vineyard. He agreed to pay them the regular wage, a silver coin a day, and sent them to work in his vineyard. He went out again to the marketplace at nine o'clock and saw some men standing there doing nothing, so he told them, 'You also go and work in the vineyard, and I will pay you a fair wage.' So they went. Then at twelve o'clock and again at three o'clock he did the same thing. It was nearly five o'clock when he went to the marketplace and saw some other men still standing there. 'Why are you wasting the whole day here doing nothing?' he asked them. 'No one hired us,' they answered. 'Well, then, you go and work in the vineyard,' he told them.

"When evening came, the owner told his foreman, 'Call the workers and pay them their wages, starting with those who were hired last and ending with those who were hired first.' The men who had begun to work at five o'clock were paid a silver coin each. So when the men who were the first to be hired came to be paid, they thought they would get more; but they too were given a silver coin each. They took their money and started grumbling against the employer. 'These men who were hired last worked only one hour,' they said, 'while we put up with a whole day's work in the hot sun—yet you paid them the same as you paid us!' 'Listen, friend,' the owner answered one of them, 'I have not cheated you. After all, you agreed to do a day's work for one silver coin. Now take your pay and go home. I want to give this man who was hired last as much as I gave you. Don't I have the right to do as I wish with my own money? Or are you jealous because I am generous?'"

And Jesus concluded, "So those who are last will be first, and those who are first will be last."

Matthew 20:1–16

ANDREW GREELEY COMMENTS

The crowd that followed Jesus loved stories. Who doesn't love stories? They were often disconcerted and sometimes angered by his stories, especially when, as in the story of the vineyard laborers, he gave familiar stories a different twist at the end. The crowd knew this story very well. They had heard it often and were reassured by it. At the end of the story, as they knew it, those who came at the eleventh hour worked so hard that they earned a full day's pay. But Jesus threw them a curve ball: instead of the emphasis being on the hard work of the late-comers it was on the generosity of the farmer. Those who went to work at the eleventh hour hardly did any work at all, they were so busy trying to figure out what the farmer would pay them. By human standards the farmer was crazy. The parable, however, is not about labor-management relations, nor about justice in human relationships. It is rather about God. Its rifle-shot point is that God is so generous and so loving that by human standards he'd be judged to be crazy. It is a parable about the insanity of God's love.

✠ A Christian Story

Once upon a time, long, long ago, there was a village up in the mountains. In the early part of summer a young man came up the mountain playing a happy little tune on a flute. The kids followed after him. He played music for them and sang songs and told stories. Pretty soon the teenagers joined him and he taught them some new dances. That night he announced that he was going to produce a play and invited the villagers to try out for him. The next night he had a song fest, and the night after that a storytelling contest, and the night after that a big dance for all ages. The people in the village never had enjoyed summer nights so much. Husbands and wives stopped quarreling; kids stopped lying to their parents, lovers were gentle with each other. All the villagers were astonished by the charm and the talent and the generosity of the young man. But after a couple of weeks the people in the village who complained about everything began to complain about the young man. Who was he? Where did he come from? Who was his family? Why did he have so much free time in the summer? What was he up to? What kind of trick was he trying to play on them? Soon the people in the village ignored him or insulted him. Parents forbade their children to go near him. Teens threw rocks at him. One night a bunch of young toughs beat him up and threw him out of town. Rumors spread that he was dead. But early in the morning the village heard the flute again, this time playing a sad little tune as the young man who was too generous walked back down the mountain.

Sloth

CHAPTER 6

A Judaic Story

R Dosa b. Harkinas says: Sleeping late in the morning, drinking wine at noon, chatting with children, and attending the synagogues of the ignorant drive a man out of the world.

Sleeping late in the morning: how so?

This teaches that a person should not intend to sleep until the time of reciting the Shema has passed.

For when someone sleeps until the time for reciting the Shema has passed, he turns out to waste time that should be spent studying the Torah.

As it is said: The lazy one says, There is a lion in the way, yes, a lion is in the streets. The door is turning on its hinges and the lazy man is still in bed.

Drinking wine at noon: how so?

This teaches that someone should not plan to drink wine at noon.

For when someone drinks wine at noon, he turns out to waste time that should be spent studying the Torah.

As it is said: Woe to you, O land, when your king is a boy and your princes feast in the morning.

And further: Happy are you, O land, when your king is a free man, and your princes eat in due season, in strength and not in drunkenness.

What is the meaning of in due season? One must say, this refers to the coming age, as it is said: I the Lord will hasten it in its time.

And further: After a lapse of time like this shall it be said of Jacob and of Israel, O what God has done.

So did the Holy One, blessed be he, say to the wicked Balaam, "After a period of time like this—but not now, not while you are standing among them, but at the time that I am going to carry out redemption for Israel [then will their king be free and prophecy be restored]."

Chatting with children: how so?

This teaches that a person should not plan to sit by himself and repeat traditions at home.

For if someone sits by himself and repeats traditions at home, he chats with his children and dependents and turns out to waste time that should be spent in the study of the Torah.

For it is said: This book of the Torah shall not depart out of your mouth, but you shall meditate in it day and night.

And attending the synagogues of the ignorant drives a man out of the world: how so?

This teaches that a person should not plan to join with the idle in the corners of the marketplace.

For if someone sits around with the idle in the corners of the marketplace, he turns out to waste time that he should spend in studying the Torah.

For so it is said: Happy is the one who has not walked in the counsel of the wicked, stood in the way of the sinners, or sat in the seat of the scornful . . . but his delight is in the Torah of the Lord.

R. Meir says, "What is the meaning of the statement, sat in the seat of the scornful?

"This refers to the theaters and circuses of the gentiles, in which people are sentenced to death, as it is said: I hate the gathering of evildoers and will not sit with the wicked.

"The word evildoers refers only to the wicked, as it is said: For the evildoers shall be cut off, and yet a little while and the wicked is no more.

"And what will be the form of the punishment that is coming to them in time to come?

"For behold the day comes, it burns as a furnace, and all the proud and all that do wickedness shall be stubble."

"And the proud are only the scorners, as it is said: A proud and haughty man—scorner is his name."

The Fathers according to Rabbi Nathan XXI:I–V

JACOB NEUSNER COMMENTS

Laziness wastes life. It is a form of self-indulgence, and in the end it ruins all ambition and denies all hope. It comes about through a variety of other sins, ignorance of the Torah, gluttony and intemperance, and the like.

A Judaic Story

Our rabbis have taught on Tannaite authority:

The poor man, rich man, and wicked man come to judgment.

To the poor man they say, "How come you did not engage in Torah study?"

If he says, "I was poor and preoccupied with earning my living," they say to him, "Were you ever poorer than Hillel?"

They said concerning Hillel the Elder that every day he would work as a day laborer and earn a tropaic. Half he paid for tuition to the bursar at the house of study, the other half he spent for food for himself and his family.

One time he did not find day labor and the bursar did not let him enter. He climbed up and suspended himself and took up his seat at the mouth of the skylight to hear the words of the living God from the very mouth of Shemaiah and Abtalion.

They say: That day was the eve of the Sabbath Friday, in the winter solstice, and it snowed on him from heaven.

At dawn said Shemaiah to Abtalion, "My brother, Abtalion, every day the house is illuminated by dawn's early light, but today it's gloomy. Is it possibly a cloudy day?"

They looked intently and recognized the shape of a man over the skylight. They went up and found him covered with three cubits of snow.

They took him down, bathed him and anointed him and set him by the fire and said, "A man such as this is worthy that the Sabbath should be profaned on his account."

To the rich man they say, "How come you did not engage in Torah study?"

If he says, "I was rich and preoccupied with managing my funds," they say to him, "Were you ever richer than R. Eleazar?"

They said concerning R. Eleazar b. Harsom that his father left him as his estate a thousand towns on shore and, correspondingly, a thousand ships at sea. And every day he would take a sack of flour on his shoulder for his sustenance and wander from town to town and city to city to learn Torah.

One time his workers found him but did not know who he was and seized him for the corvée. He said to them, "Please let me be, so that I may go and study Torah."

They said to him, "By the life of R. Eleazar b. Harsom, we shall not let you go."

That was because in his entire life he had never seen them, because he remained in session all day and all night, engaged with the Torah.

To the wicked person they say, "How come you did not engage in Torah study?"

If he says, "I was good-looking and preoccupied with fulfilling my sexual desires," they say to him, "Were you better looking than Joseph?"

They said concerning Joseph, that righteous man, that every day the wife of Potiphar would try to seduce him with words. Not only so, but the garment that she put on for him in the morning she did not wear by night, and the garments that she put on for him by night she did not put on for him in the morning.

She said to him, "Submit to me."

He said to her, "No."

She said to him, "Then I'll put you in prison."

He said to her, "The Lord frees the bound."

She said to him, "Then I'll cut you down to size."

He said to her, " 'The Lord raises up those who are bowed down.' "

She said to him, "Then I'll blind your eyes."

He said to her, " 'The Lord opens the eyes of the blind.' "

She gave him a thousand talents of silver to submit to her, to lie with her, to be with her, but he did not want to submit to her,

> "to lie with her—in this world,
> to be with her, in the world to come."

It turns out that Hillel serves to convict the poor, R. Eleazar b. Harsom the rich, and Joseph the wicked.

Bavli Yoma 3:7/35B

JACOB NEUSNER COMMENTS

Wealth, poverty, and Torah study all are linked to the matter of sloth. The best use of time and energy, the best form of labor, brings a person to study the Torah, so failure to study the Torah embodies sloth. Hence sages take up the matter of excuses for sloth, by pointing to how saints and sages, in order to study the Torah, overcame poverty, wealth, and the impulse to do evil.

✚ *A Gospel Story*

"Now, what do you think? There was once a man who had two sons. He went to the older one and said, 'Son, go and work in the vineyard today.' 'I don't want to,' he answered, but later he changed his mind and went. Then the father went to the other son and said the same thing. 'Yes, sir,' he answered, but he did not go. Which one of the two did what his father wanted?"

"The older one," they answered.

So Jesus said to them, "I tell you: the tax collectors and the prostitutes are going into the Kingdom of God ahead of you. For John the Baptist came to you showing you the right path to take, and you would not believe him; but the tax collectors and the prostitutes believed him. Even when you saw this, you did not later change your minds and believe him."

Matthew 21:28–32

ANDREW GREELEY COMMENTS

This Gospel story is the first of three parables of judgment upon the religious foes of Jesus. The parables continue Matthew's emphasis on Jesus and his preaching as the crucial moment in Israel's history. This parable can be viewed from a number of perspectives. First of all, the gospel is preached and heard by sinners and outcasts and rejected by the religious establishment. We also find the hypocrisy of the religious person who says one thing and does another. In addition, verses 31–32 link Jesus with John the Baptist, who also urged repentance and was rejected by the religious leaders but accepted by tax collectors and harlots.

✠ *A Christian Story*

Once upon a time, not so very long ago, there were two sisters who were the neighborhood baby-sitters. One evening the new couple on the block hired the younger sister to baby-sit for their children. When they returned home, the house was a mess, the sitter was half asleep on the couch, and they could see that the children had not followed their routine of washing up and brushing their teeth. The next morning, the children were so excited. They told their parents how the sitter had played with them and told them wonderful stories and run races with them and helped them say their prayers before they went to sleep. Still, the parents decided they would not use a sitter who left such a mess again. The next time they went out, they hired the older sister. When they returned home this time, the house was neat and orderly, the children asleep, the baby-sitter at the table studying. She reported that the children had been angels and there were no problems. They were very pleased with her and gave her an extra tip. The next morning the children complained that the sitter had yelled at them using swear words, made them play outside after dark while she talked to her boyfriend on the phone, made them go to bed early, and then went outside and smoked and talked with some friends. Which of the two sitters would you want to use?

✠ *A Gospel Story*

At that time Jesus said, "Father, Lord of heaven and earth! I thank you because you have shown to the unlearned what you have hidden from the wise and learned. Yes, Father, this was how you were pleased to have it happen.

"My Father has given me all things. No one knows the Son except the Father, and no one knows the Father except the Son and those to whom the Son chooses to reveal him.

"Come to me, all of you who are tired from carrying heavy loads, and I will give you rest. Take my yoke and put it on you, and learn from me, because I am gentle and humble in spirit; and you will find rest. For the yoke I will give you is easy, and the load I will put on you is light."

Matthew 11:25–30

ANDREW GREELEY COMMENTS

In this Gospel passage St. Matthew continues his "logical" organization of the words and deeds of Jesus by topics or by similarity of words. The related topics in this passage are the expression of Jesus' concern for little children and his love for us as members of his family. The latter passage in which he says that his yoke is easy and his burden is light does not seem to fit the reality of our lives. The yoke is often hard and the burden is heavy. Jesus obviously means that if we can identify with the love of God that he experiences, life will look very different. Alas, it is so hard to do that.

✝ *A Christian Story*

Once upon a time there was a boss and an administrative assistant. The AA was not the most ambitious or reliable person in the world, but he tried hard at least some of the time. The boss was generous and good-hearted because it was in her nature to be so. When she corrected his mistakes, she did so very gently. When holidays fell in the middle of the week, she gave him the rest of the days off. She gave him the week after Christmas off because, as she said, nothing ever gets done that week anyhow. On summer Fridays she let him go home at noon. Whenever he needed time off to go to the doctor or for some family event, she gave it to him without question. She granted him a substantial raise every year and wrote generous reports on him to the personnel office. Finally, he saw what he thought would be a better job and quit without notice. He told the new AA, "You won't like working for her, she's too demanding."

Gluttony

CHAPTER 7

S aid R. Aha, "There is the case of a man who sold all his household goods to buy wine with the proceeds, the very beams of his house to buy wine with the proceeds.

"His children complained, saying, 'Will this old man of ours leave the world without leaving us a thing after he dies? What can we do with him? Let's go and make him drink and get him drunk and put him on a slab and take him out and say he's dead and lay him on his bier in the graveyard.' They did just that, taking him and getting him drunk and bringing him out and leaving him in the cemetery.

"Wine merchants passed by the gate of the graveyard. They heard that the corvée tax of personal service to the crown was being levied in that town. They said, 'Come and let's unload the wineskins in this grave and get out of here.' That's just what they did. They unloaded their burdens in the cemetery and went off to find out about the uproar in the town. Now that man was lying there, and the merchants saw him and took for granted that he was dead.

"When the man woke up from his sleep, he saw a skin of wine hanging above his head. He untied it and put the spout in his mouth and drank. When he was feeling good, he began to sing. After three days, his children said to one another,

'Shouldn't we go and see how father's doing—whether he's alive or dead!'

"They came and found him with a wineskin spout in his mouth, and he was sitting and drinking. They said to him, 'Even here your Creator has not abandoned you among the dead, but he has left you among the living. Since this is what Heaven has meted out to you, we don't know what we can do for you.' They agreed among themselves to provide for him and arrange some sort of permanent provision for him. They set things up so that each one would provide him with a drink per day."

It is written, "You will be like one who lies down in the midst of the sea, like one who lies on the top of a mast. 'They struck me,' you will say, 'but I was not hurt; they beat me, but I did not feel it. When shall I awake? I will seek another drink.'"

"You will be like one who lies down in the midst of the sea": like a boat tossed on the high seas, going down and up, down and up.

Just as a ship is shaken in the ocean, so in the end a habitual drunkard is shaken out of his wits.

Leviticus Rabbah XII:I.1 = Esther Rabbah I XXXII:i.1

Said R. Yudan, "During the entire seven-year period in which Solomon built the house of the sanctuary, he did not drink any wine.

"When he had built the house of the sanctuary, and in celebration married Pharaoh's daughter, that very night he drank some wine.

"There were two dances in celebration that night, one, the rejoicing over the building of the house of the sanctuary, and the other, the rejoicing over the daughter of Pharaoh.

"Said the Holy One, blessed be he, 'Which one shall I accept, this or that?'

"At that moment it entered God's mind to destroy the Temple.

"That is in line with the following verse of Scripture: 'This city has aroused my anger and wrath from the day it was built to this day, so that I will remove it from my sight because of all the evil of the sons of Israel and the sons of Judah, which they did to provoke me to anger.'"

Leviticus Rabbah XII:V.1

JACOB NEUSNER COMMENTS

So far as sages were concerned, the most deplorable form of gluttony is drunkenness. Indeed, some sages held that the forbidden fruit of the Garden of Eden was the vine. They regarded alcoholism as a major problem in the life of the holy people, Israel, and they further regarded gluttony in the form of dunkenness as the source of Israel's straying after idols. That is why they focused on the discussion of the dangers of drink in presenting their teachings on the matter.

✠ *A Gospel Story*

At once the Spirit made him [Jesus] go into the desert, where he stayed forty days, being tempted by Satan. Wild animals were there also, but angels came and helped him.

After John had been put in prison, Jesus went to Galilee and preached the Good News from God. "The right time has come," he said, "and the Kingdom of God is near! Turn away from your sins and believe the Good News!"

Mark 1:12–15

ANDREW GREELEY COMMENTS

It is interesting to note how jejune Mark's Gospel about the fast and the temptation is when compared with the later Gospels. It is not unreasonable to think that the later Gospels are theological embroidering on the older tradition. For St. Mark the theme of the story is the close link between the preparation in the desert and the beginning of Jesus' preaching. He went forth to tell men and women that God's love was near only after he prepared himself by focusing his energies on the work that was ahead.

✠ *A Christian Story*

Once upon a time there was a husband and wife who had grown up after Lenten fasting was abolished. They had never heard of such a thing till it was mentioned once in a study group at their parish. Those in the study group who remembered the fast said, "Thank heaven we don't have to do it anymore." Those who did not remember said, "What a silly idea that was; thank heaven we never had to do it."

Our friends asked the priest, "Why did they fast?"

The priest said, "Because Jesus did."

"Why did Jesus fast?" they asked.

"To prepare himself for his mission."

"Oh," they said.

"The Moslems still do it," the priest said. "Remember when Hakim couldn't eat before a basketball game? But they can eat all they want for supper."

"You can't lose much weight doing that," our couple said. The priest agreed. "Of course," he said, "they have to give up marital love too."

Our friends said, "No way we Catholics ever did that." Everyone laughed, some of them a bit uneasily. Our friends went home.

"What's the big reason for not wanting to do it any more?" the wife asked.

"Everyone fasts," the husband said, "to lose weight; why not do it to strengthen our focus and give us religious reason for losing weight?"

"Let's!" said the wife. "But we won't tell any of our friends," the husband said, "because they'll think we're crazy for using religious faith to lose weight."

✠ *A Gospel Story*

The next day John was standing there again with two of his disciples, when he saw Jesus walking by. "There is the Lamb of God!" he said.

The two disciples heard him say this and went with Jesus. Jesus turned, saw them following him, and asked, "What are you looking for?"

They answered, "Where do you live, Rabbi?" (This word means "Teacher.")

"Come and see," he answered. (It was then about four o'clock in the afternoon.) So they went with him and saw where he lived, and spent the rest of that day with him.

One of them was Andrew, Simon Peter's brother. At once he found his brother Simon and told him, "We have found the Messiah." (This word means "Christ.") Then he took Simon to Jesus.

Jesus looked at him and said, "Your name is Simon son of John, but you will be called Cephas." (This is the same as Peter and means "a rock.")

John 1:35–42

ANDREW GREELEY COMMENTS

Jesus had peculiar taste in friends. You put the whole crowd together and they were not as smart as one of the third-rate philosophers in Rome. Maybe some of them could read and write. They were perhaps street smart, but if you were going to announce the nearness of the kingdom of God, would you surround yourself with folks who wouldn't make assistant precinct captain? They were utterly insensitive to Jesus' spiritual message and interested only in the power and prestige they were going to have in his kingdom (which they didn't understand at all). One of them was a thief and ten of them were cowards. Surely, even if he had decided to limit his choice to Galilee, Jesus could have done better? Why these sluggards and nerds? Why indeed? And why do we pretend that our church leaders today are better than they were? Patently the first pope and the first bishops (if we want to use that analogy) were not sacred persons, but inept, often stupid human beings. Why do we have to pretend that their successors are any better? Why should they be immune from criticism? Have we missed the point somewhere along the line that the leaders of the church and the followers in the church are fragile, imperfect human beings and that Jesus chose them precisely because he wanted a human church? If he wanted something better, he should have turned it over, not to the philosophers in Rome, but to the Seraphim.

✠ A Christian Story

Once upon a time there was a group of young men who idolized the quarterback on the local NFL team. He was a great passer and a gutsy runner, he played despite pain, he was modest at media interviews, generous with volunteer work, kind to kids, and signed autographs till all had been accommodated. He was humble and respectful and prayed before every game. He was all but perfect, it seemed, a great role model for kids in the city and around the country.

Then one night he came into the tavern where these young men hung out. He was roaring drunk and abusive. He pushed a couple of women around, insulted the bartender, picked a fight with a little guy, and sneered at our group of idolaters. They were shocked into silence. However, one of them—a bit of a nerd—actually asked the quarterback for his autograph. Their hero cursed him out and knocked the pen out of his hand.

"What a jerk," they all said. "We won't cheer for him ever again. He's a disgrace. No role model for children at all. He probably uses drugs too."

The nerd who asked for the autograph said, "But he's human like the rest of us. We all make mistakes, don't we?"

"We're not supposed to be role models," his friends said.

PART II

The Seven Virtues

CHAPTER 8

✠ A Gospel Story

T hen Jesus told his disciples a parable to teach them that they should always pray and never become discouraged. "In a certain town there was a judge who neither feared God nor respected people. And there was a widow in that same town who kept coming to him and pleading for her rights, saying, 'Help me against my opponent!' For a long time the judge refused to act, but at last he said to himself, 'Even though I don't fear God or respect people, yet because of all the trouble this widow is giving me, I will see to it that she gets her rights. If I don't, she will keep on coming and finally wear me out!'"

And the Lord continued, "Listen to what that corrupt judge said. Now, will God not judge in favor of his own people who cry to him day and night for help? Will he be slow to help them? I tell you, he will judge in their favor and do it quickly. But will the Son of Man find faith on earth when he comes?"

Luke 18:1–8

ANDREW GREELEY COMMENTS

The parables of Jesus are like a flash of light in the darkness, a thunderclap on a clear summer day. They are disconcerting stories with only one point that is made quickly and decisively, if mysteriously. They usually shocked those who heard them. If they do not shock us now, the reason is perhaps that we have heard them so often that the "strangeness" of the imagery of the story—such as the comparison of God with an unjust judge—is lost. In general there are two kinds of parables, those which are designed to encourage and reassure us and those intended to give us a sense of urgency, of the need to act while there is yet time. Today's story clearly belongs to the former category. There are a number of problems in understanding the (sword)thrust of a parable, of which two must be kept in mind always: (1) The early church often modified the thrust somewhat to fit an issue or a problem it faced. (2) The Gospel writers often added to the story words from another part of the tradition with which they were working because the same words are found in both parts of the tradition even though the pericopes are not logically connected. Thus in today's Gospel, the second paragraph, or at least the last three sentences of it, is not part of the original story presented in the first paragraph.

✠ *A Christian Story*

Once upon a time there was a parish priest who hated teenagers. He absolutely refused to permit them to use the parish premises for anything. Finally everyone gave up and went to other parishes. But when Molly Whupi (a character from Celtic mythology who often appears in my stories) was a freshman in high school, she and her friends and their boys hung out in front of the rectory every day and pestered the poor priest every time they saw him.

Finally he gave in. "A real teenage club wouldn't bother me any more than you kids do. But please don't destroy the rectory on me."

And you know what Molly Whupi said? She said, "We bother God even more than we bother you."

✠ *A Gospel Story*

Then Jesus made the disciples get into the boat and go on ahead to the other side of the lake, while he sent the people away. After sending the people away, he went up a hill by himself to pray. When evening came, Jesus was there alone, and by this time the boat was far out on the lake, tossed about by the waves, because the wind was blowing against it.

Between three and six o'clock in the morning Jesus came to the disciples, walking on the water. When they saw him walking on the water, they were terrified. "It's a ghost!" they said, and screamed with fear.

Jesus spoke to them at once. "Courage!" he said. "It is I. Don't be afraid!"

Then Peter spoke up. "Lord, if it is really you, order me to come out on the water to you."

"Come!" answered Jesus. So Peter got out of the boat and started walking on the water to Jesus. But when he noticed the strong wind, he was afraid and started to sink down in the water. "Save me, Lord!" he cried.

At once Jesus reached out and grabbed hold of him and said, "What little faith you have! Why did you doubt?"

They both got into the boat, and the wind died down. Then the disciples in the boat worshiped Jesus. "Truly you are the Son of God!" they exclaimed.

Matthew 14:22–33

ANDREW GREELEY COMMENTS

This story was intended for those followers of Jesus who were worried about the possibility of government persecutions, opposition from other religious groups, and the very slow (as it seemed) progress of Christianity. The story says that, as President Roosevelt said when he was inaugurated in 1933, the only thing we have to fear is fear itself, blind unreasoning terror that paralyzes our every action. While the story was told to reassure the very early Christians, it applies to us as much as it did to them.

✠ *A Christian Story*

Once upon a time there was a high school physics teacher who gave very tough tests. But he was also a good teacher and liked his students and wanted them to learn. So he emphasized the really important parts of the course and prepared the students for the exam. He even told them that if they listened carefully in class they would know what the final exam would be about. But the students didn't really believe him. So they took copious notes of everything he said and the words passed from his lectures to their notes, without pausing in their memories. When the time came for the test, most of the students went into an advanced stage of panic. They knew that their physics grade would be very important when it came time to apply for college. So they studied like crazy, pored over their notes, and even had study sessions in which groups of students would try to study together—with rock music in the background of course, because teenagers can't study without music in the background. Three of the kids didn't study at all because they hadn't taken any notes. They went to the movies the night before the test. The test was truly fearsome. The three who hadn't studied finished in a half hour and walked out of class confidently. The rest of the class went into a wild hysteria. They forgot everything about physics they ever knew. Most of them flunked. A few ended up with Ds. "Why didn't you listen to what I said," the teacher asked, "O you of little faith?"

✡ *A Judaic Story*

R. Gamaliel, R. Joshua, R. Eleazar b. Azariah, and R. Aqiba were going toward Rome. They heard the sound of the city's traffic from as far away as Puteoli, a hundred and twenty miles away. They began to cry, while R. Aqiba laughed.

They said to him, "Aqiba, why are we crying while you are laughing?"

He said to them, "Why are you crying?"

They said to him, "Should we not cry, since gentiles, idolators, sacrifice to their idols and bow down to icons, but dwell securely in prosperity, serenely, while the house of the footstool of our God has been put to the torch and left a lair for beasts of the field?"

He said to them, "That is precisely why I was laughing. If this is how he has rewarded those who anger him, all the more so will he reward those who do his will."

Another time they went up to Jerusalem and went to Mount Scopus. They tore their garments.

They came to the mountain of the house of the Temple and saw a fox go forth from the house of the holy of holies. They began to cry, while R. Aqiba laughed.

They said to him, "You are always giving surprises. We are crying when you laugh!"

He said to them, "But why are you crying?"

They said to him, "Should we not cry over the place concerning which it is written, 'And the common person who draws near shall be put to death'? Now lo, a fox comes out of it.

"In our connection the following verse of Scripture has been carried out: 'For this our heart is faint, for these things our eyes are dim, for the mountain of Zion which is desolate, the foxes walk upon it.'"

He said to them, "That is the very reason I have laughed. For lo, it is written, 'And I will take for me faithful witnesses to record, Uriah the priest and Zechariah the son of Jeberechiah.'

"And what has Uriah got to do with Zechariah? What is it that Uriah said? 'Zion shall be plowed as a field and Jerusalem shall become heaps and the mountain of the Lord's house as the high places of a forest.'

"What is it that Zechariah said? 'Thus says the Lord of hosts, "Old men and women shall yet sit in the broad places of Jerusalem."'

"Said the Omnipresent, 'Lo, I have these two witnesses. If the words of Uriah have been carried out, then the words of

Zechariah will be carried out. If the words of Uriah are nullified, then the words of Zechariah will be nullified.'

"Therefore I was happy that the words of Uriah have been
carried out, so that in the end the words of Zechariah will
come about."

In this language they replied to him: "Aqiba, you have
given us comfort."

Sifré to Deuteronomy XLIII:III

JACOB NEUSNER COMMENTS

Faith stands for two matters, faith *that*, and faith *in*, meaning
trust. Faith *that* is propositional, as in, "I believe in perfect faith
that the Messiah will come," one of the thirteen principles
of faith put forward by the great sage Moses Maimonides
(1135–1204). Faith *in* speaks of trust, as in the statement, "I
have faith in God, that he will save me." It is this second sense
of the word faith that comes to the fore in the stories that sages
tell about having faith in God's promises through the prophets
in the ultimate salvation of Israel, the holy people.

♈ *A Judaic Story*

R. Judah said Rab said, "At the time that Moses went up on
high, he found the Holy One in session, affixing crowns to the
letters of the words of the Torah. He said to him, 'Lord of the
Universe, who is stopping you from regarding the document
as perfect without these additional crowns on the letters?'

"He said to him, 'There is a man who is going to arrive at
the end of many generations, and Aqiba b. Joseph is his name,
who is going to interpret on the basis of each point of the
crowns heaps and heaps of laws.'

"He said to him, 'Lord of the Universe, show him to me.'

"He said to him, 'Turn around.'

"He went and took a seat at the end of eight rows, but he
could not grasp what the people were saying. He felt faint. But
when the discourse reached a certain matter, and the disciples

said, 'My lord, how do you know this?' and he answered, 'It is a law given to Moses from Sinai,' he regained his composure.

"He went and came before the Holy One. He said before him, 'Lord of the Universe, how come you have someone like that and yet you give the Torah through me?'

"He said to him, 'Silence! That is how the thought came to me.'

"He said to him, 'Lord of the Universe, you have shown me his Torah, now show me his reward.'

"He said to him, 'Turn around.'

"He turned around and saw his flesh being weighed out at the butcher-stalls in the market.

"He said to him, 'Lord of the Universe, 'Such is Torah, such is the reward?'

"He said to him, 'Silence! That is how the thought came to me.'"

Bavli Menahot 29b

JACOB NEUSNER COMMENTS

Faith requires the attitude that though we do not understand, yet we must accept God's will. In the end it is that kind of faith that forms the center of this narrative, one of the most profound and difficult stories that the ancient Judaic sages ever told. It draws the contrast between the greatness of a sage of the Torah, Aqiba, and the fate that God meted out to him. Contrasting with sages' conviction that God's justice shows itself in the end, this story insists that, even when we do not understand, we still have to accept in perfect faith God's decision.

Hope

CHAPTER 9

✠ *A Gospel Story*

When Jesus heard the news about John, he left there in a boat and went to a lonely place by himself. The people heard about it, and so they left their towns and followed him by land. Jesus got out of the boat, and when he saw the large crowd, his heart was filled with pity for them, and he healed their sick. That evening his disciples came to him and said, "It is already very late, and this is a lonely place. Send the people away and let them go to the villages to buy food for themselves."

"They don't have to leave," answered Jesus. "You yourselves give them something to eat!"

"All we have here are five loaves and two fish," they replied.

"Then bring them here to me," Jesus said. He ordered the people to sit down on the grass; then he took the five loaves and the two fish, looked up to heaven, and gave thanks to God. He broke the loaves and gave them to the disciples, and the disciples gave them to the people. Everyone ate and had enough. Then the disciples took up twelve baskets full of what was left over. The number of men who ate was about five thousand, not counting the women and children.

Matthew 14:13–21

ANDREW GREELEY COMMENTS

There are two versions of this story in Matthew's Gospel, a phenomenon that scripture scholars call "doubling." The author of the Gospel doubtless had a number of different sources in front of him as he worked, most notably St. Mark's Gospel and a collection of the "sayings" of Jesus (like "Many are called, but few are chosen"). He also had available other traditions. Rather than leave something out, he chose to include two slightly different versions of the same stories. We must remember that these written sources with which the author worked had been preceded by oral traditions, though it now seems likely that the traditions were reduced to writing early in the development of Christianity. The story of the multiplication of the loaves and fishes is eucharistic in its intent. Some clergy agonize over whether the miracle was an actual physical multiplication or merely a result of everyone bringing forth their small supplies of food. But this misses the point of the story—that God feeds us with both ordinary food and with the Eucharist, which unites us with Herself in a banquet of love.

✠ *A Christian Story*

Once a mother took a course in cooking pastries. She learned how to make the most delightful sweet rolls and cakes and pies and tortes and fancy French goodies that would make your mouth water when you saw them. One Sunday she made raisin Danish for breakfast, Linzer tortes for lunch, and a wonderful white chocolate mousse for supper. But her husband and kids were boors when it came to food. All they wanted was chocolate-coated Dunkin' Donuts. So the mother, who loved her husband and children, bought chocolate coated Dunkin' Donuts the next Sunday. She also made her wonderful pastries and brought them over to the rectory for the priests!

✠ *A Gospel Story*

"Do not be worried and upset," Jesus told them. "Believe in God and believe also in me. There are many rooms in my Father's house, and I am going to prepare a place for you. I would not tell you this if it were not so. And after I go and prepare a place for you, I will come back and take you to myself, so that you will be where I am. You know the way that leads to the place where I am going."

Thomas said to him, "Lord, we do not know where you are going; so how can we know the way to get there?"

Jesus answered him, "I am the way, the truth, and the life; no one goes to the Father except by me. Now that you have known me," he said to them, "you will know my Father also, and from now on you do know him and you have seen him."

Philip said to him, "Lord, show us the Father; that is all we need."

Jesus answered, "For a long time I have been with you all; yet you do not know me, Philip? Whoever has seen me has seen the Father. Why, then, do you say, 'Show us the Father'? Do you not believe, Philip, that I am in the Father and the Father is in me? The words that I have spoken to you," Jesus said to his disciples, "do not come from me. The Father, who remains in me, does his own work. Believe me when I say that I am in the Father and the Father is in me. If not, believe because of the things I do. I am telling you the truth; those who believe in me will do what I do—yes, they will do even greater things, because I am going to the Father.

John 14:1–12

ANDREW GREELEY COMMENTS

The "last supper" discourse is in chapters 14, 15, and 16 of St. John's Gospel. While this long mystical and theological meditation on Jesus, his life, his work, and his relationship with his followers is placed in John's narrative before the arrest and execution of Jesus, it in fact can be considered most fully in light of the experience of Jesus which the early Christians had, an experience of the Jesus who was once dead as now alive again and in active communion with them. It reveals the enormous affection Jesus had for his friends and companions, his great care and concern for them, the need for him to leave them behind, and his guarantee that, despite the separation, he would always be with them. This experience of Jesus surely went back to the very beginning, though John's soaring rhetoric is a well-developed reflection on that experience. While it is difficult for us to comprehend all that John is trying to say, it is easy enough to grasp that this Gospel story is about his passionate affection for his companions—and for us.

✠ A Christian Story

Once upon a time a great leader decided that he had ruled his country long enough. He was still in the prime of life, but he had lost his wife, his son was old enough to succeed him, and the leader wanted to spend the rest of his time on earth in a monastery reading and writing, praying and reflecting. Truth to tell, he was tired of the world, tired of the burdens of office, tired of the distractions of daily life. He called his family and his advisers and his poets together and told them that it was time he stepped down. He had ruled long enough. He was growing rusty and stale on the job. It was time for new leadership, new blood, new ideas, new vision. Everyone protested, most of all the crown prince, who felt utterly inadequate to replace his father. The leader understood their reaction and was deeply moved by it. But he said it was time for him to withdraw, time for his family and friends to be on their own. He had done his part in reorganizing the country and making it peaceful and prosperous; now it was their turn to take over and stand for all the things he had stood for during his life. "I'll always be with you," he said. "And if you ever need help—and I don't think you will—I will come back. But it is time for you to become mature, to act like adults, to lead in my name but without me."

Jesus is giving us the same message. It is time for us to be confident adult Christians.

🕎 *Judaic Stories*

Our rabbis have taught on Tannaite authority:

To him who gives his fellow the benefit of the doubt, they give the benefit of the doubt. And there was the case of someone who came down from Upper Galilee and was employed by someone in the South for three years. On the eve of the Day of Atonement he said to him, "Pay me my wages so that I can go and feed my wife and children."

He said to him, "I don't have any ready cash."

He said to him, "Then pay me in produce."

He said to him, "I don't have any."

"Give me land."

"I don't have any."

"Give me cattle."

"I don't have any."

"Give me pillows and blankets."

"I don't have any."

So he tossed his things over his shoulder and went home depressed. After the festival the householder took the man's salary in hand and with it three loaded asses, one bearing food, another drink, the third, various goodies, and he went to the man's house. After they had eaten and drunk, he gave him his salary. He said to him, "When you said to me, 'Give me my wages,' and I said to you, 'I don't have any ready cash,' of what did you suspect me?"

"I thought that you might have come upon a real bargain to buy with the cash."

"And when you said to me, 'Give me cattle,' and I said to you, 'I don't have cattle,' of what did you suspect me?"

"I thought that it might have been hired out to third parties."

"When you said to me, 'Give me land,' and I said to you, 'I don't have any land,' of what did you suspect me?"

"I thought that it might have been sharecropped by a third party."

"And when I said to you, 'I don't have produce,' of what did you suspect me?"

"I thought that they might not be tithed."

"And when I said to you, 'I don't have pillows and blankets,' of what did you suspect me?"

"I thought that you might have sanctified all your property to Heaven."

He said to him, "By the Temple service! That's just how things were. I vowed all my property to others on account of my son, Hyrcanus, who does not engage in Torah study, and when I went to my fellows in the South, they released me from my vow, and you, just as you gave me the benefit of the doubt, may the Omnipresent give you the benefit of the doubt."

❧

Our rabbis have taught on Tannaite authority:

There was the case of a certain pious man who ransomed an Israelite woman from kidnappers. At the inn he had her lie at his feet. In the morning he went down, immersed, and repeated Torah traditions to his disciples.

He said to them, "When I had her lie down at my feet, of what did you suspect me?"

They said, "Perhaps among us is a disciple who is not thoroughly known by the master."

"When I went down and immersed, of what did you suspect me?"

"We thought that because of the rigors of the journey the master may have had a seminal emission."

He said to them, "By the Temple service! That's just how things were. Just as you gave me the benefit of the doubt, may the Omnipresent give you the benefit of the doubt."

❧

Our rabbis have taught on Tannaite authority:
Once, disciples of sages needed something from a Roman

courtesan, with whom all the great men of Rome were intimate. They said, "Who will go?"

Said to them R. Joshua, "I will go."

R. Joshua and his disciples went. When they got to the door of her house, he took off his phylacteries at a distance of four cubits and went in and locked the door before them. When he came out, he went down and immersed and then he repeated Torah traditions for his disciples. And he said to them, "When I took off my phylacteries, of what did you suspect me?"

"We thought that the master was thinking that one should not bring holy words into an unclean place."

"When I locked the door, of what did you suspect me?"

"We thought that perhaps some matter of government may be dealt with between him and her."

"When I went down and immersed, of what did you suspect me?"

"We thought, maybe a bit of spit from her mouth landed on the garments of the master."

He said to them, "By the Temple service! That's just how things were. Just as you gave me the benefit of the doubt, may the Omnipresent give you the benefit of the doubt."

Bavli to M Shab 18:2

JACOB NEUSNER COMMENTS

Faith and hope travel together; both represent attitudes of confidence despite how matters appear, the expectation that goodness can come even when this world does not give much reason to expect it. Hope stands for an attitude of confidence and trust, and for our sages, to hope means, above all, to hope in other people and to give them the benefit of every doubt. This attitude of hope is expressed in a story that carries to the extreme the notion that we must not give up on the other. But hope, like faith, in the end forms the substance of our attitude toward God; how we look upon and treat our fellow humans mirrors our attitude toward God, and that is why sages define hope, as they explain faith, by stories about everyday people and events.

Charity

CHAPTER 10

✠ *A Gospel Story*

And Jesus said, "If you love me, you will obey my commandments. I will ask the Father, and he will give you another Helper, who will stay with you forever. He is the Spirit, who reveals the truth about God. The world cannot receive him, because it cannot see him or know him. But you know him, because he remains with you and is in you.

"When I go, you will not be left all alone; I will come back to you. In a little while the world will see me no more, but you will see me; and because I live, you also will live. When that day comes, you will know that I am in my Father and that you are in me, just as I am in you.

"Those who accept my commandments and obey them are the ones who love me. My Father will love those who love me; I too will love them and reveal myself to them."

John 14:15–21

ANDREW GREELEY COMMENTS

In many Gospel stories Jesus is portrayed as being deeply reluctant to leave his followers behind. He loves them. He will miss them. He will always be with them, but not in the same way he has been. He will take care of them as best he can. He wants to reassure them, yet he cannot deny the pain of separation from which they will suffer—and by implication from which he too will suffer. He promises them that they will not be alone, that he will send another to be their inspiration and guide, the advocate, the guardian, the spirit of truth. Reading the later doctrine of the Trinity back into this passage, we recognize the promise that God's Holy Spirit will always be with the followers of Jesus. The Spirit's invisible but powerful presence will be with them until finally Jesus is reunited with them. This message was intended primarily for the early Christians who believed in Jesus but who lamented his absence. But it is also intended for us. We are not alone. No matter how bad things might seem, Jesus is still with us.

✝ *A Christian Story*

Once upon a time a woman had to travel to a city across the country on business and remain there for a week. It was only a short period, she told her husband and children. The week would pass by before they knew it. Sometimes, she said, a whole week would pass by at home and most of the members of the family would hardly say a word to her. What was the big deal about her not being in the house for a few days? Well, they agreed that she had to go away but said they didn't have to like it. She phoned them each evening while she was out of town but warned them that on one evening she wouldn't be able to do so because she would be stuck with a late dinner. She got back to her hotel at 11:30. It was 10:30 in her hometown. Too late to call. Besides, she had told them that she wouldn't call. Probably they had all gone to bed. Maybe by now they were used to her being away. She turned on the TV and saw that crazy ad where a man alone in his hotel room is talking to his wife, even though she's back home; then he reaches for the phone. And so, tears pouring down her cheeks, the woman picked up the phone and called. Guess what? Were they all in bed? Of course not. They were waiting at the phone for her to call. Everyone had a good cry, even her unemotional teenage son. That's how Jesus feels about us. When we feel that way about those we love, we bring Jesus' love to them. The mother in a distant city represented her own love and the love of Jesus.

✝ *A Gospel Story*

Jesus said, "Do not think that I have come to do away with the Law of Moses and the teachings of the prophets. I have not come to do away with them, but to make their teachings come true. Remember that as long as heaven and earth last, not the least point nor the smallest detail of the Law will be done away with—not until the end of all things. So then, whoever disobeys even the least important of the commandments and teaches others to do the same, will be least in the Kingdom of heaven. On the other hand, whoever obeys the Law and teaches others to do the same, will be great in the Kingdom of heaven. I tell you, then, that you will be able to enter the Kingdom of heaven only if you are more faithful than the teachers of the Law and the Pharisees in doing what God requires.

"You have heard that people were told in the past, 'Do not commit murder; anyone who does will be brought to trial.' But now I tell you: if you are angry with your brother you will be brought to trial, if you call your brother 'You good-for-nothing!' you will be brought before the Council, and if you call your brother a worthless fool you will be in danger of going to the fire of hell. So if you are about to offer your gift to God at the altar and there you remember that your brother has something against you, leave your gift there in front of the altar, go at once and make peace with your brother, and then come back and offer your gift to God. If someone brings a lawsuit against you and takes you to court, settle the dispute while there is time, before you get to court. Once you are there, you will be turned over to the judge, who will hand you over to the police, and you will be put in jail. There you will stay, I tell you, until you pay the last penny of your fine.

"You have heard that it was said, 'Do not commit adultery.' But now I tell you: anyone who looks at a woman and wants to possess her is guilty of committing adultery with her in his heart. So if your right eye causes you to sin, take it out and throw it away! It is much better for you to lose a part of your body than to have your whole body thrown into hell. If your right hand causes you to sin, cut it off and throw it away! It is much better for you to lose one of your limbs than to have your whole body go off to hell.

"It was also said, 'Anyone who divorces his wife must give her a written notice of divorce.' But now I tell you: if a man divorces his wife for any cause other than her unfaithfulness, then he is guilty of making her commit adultery if she marries again, and the man who marries her commits adultery also.

"You have also heard that people were told in the past, 'Do not break your promise, but do what you have vowed to the Lord to do.' But now I tell you: do not use any vow when you make a promise. Do not swear by heaven, for it is God's throne; nor by earth, for it is the resting place for his feet; nor by Jerusalem, for it is the city of the great King. Do not even swear by your head, because you cannot make a single hair white or black. Just say 'Yes' or 'No'—anything else you say comes from the Evil One.

Matthew 5:17–37

ANDREW GREELEY COMMENTS

This Gospel story illustrates how the Sermon on the Mount is a kind of mixtum-gatherum account of the teachings of Jesus. It is a collection of sayings about the Jewish law that Jesus probably spoke on different occasions. The Evangelist is trying to explain the relationship between the Jewish law and the preaching of Jesus, a problem that puzzled many in the early Christian community to whom he was writing. In effect, he says, Jesus' teachings fulfilled the law instead of replacing it. The most interesting part of the passage for us today is the segment where he speaks as a protofeminist and rejects the notion that only women can commit adultery against their spouses (a man committed adultery only against the husband of a married woman).

✠ *A Christian Story*

Once upon a time a husband and a wife had a big fight. No one was quite sure what the fight was about. Each time one or the other told the background of the fight, it changed. Then they fought about what the fight was about and what the other person had said the day before about the fight. Technically they were not talking to each other, but they could still talk enough to keep the fight going.

"Maybe I should get a divorce if you're so fed up with me," the man said.

"Fine," said his wife, "only you get the kids."

So he stopped talking about divorce. Their guardian angels had a summit conference and decided that something had to be done. They arranged for the husband's car to be bumped by a hit-and-run driver. Neither car was badly damaged, but the poor husband spent two days in the hospital under "observation." The quarrel was quickly forgotten.

The wife said, "Sometimes I think I'd be better off without you; then I face the prospect of being without you and realize I'd not be better off.

So they fell in love all over again, which is what St. Valentine's Day is supposed to be about.

♦ *Judaic Stories*

A certain ass driver appeared before the rabbis [the context requires:] in a dream, in which the driver's prayers for rain were answered. The rabbis sent and brought him and said to him, "What is your trade?"

He said to them, "I am an ass driver."

They said to him, "And how do you conduct your business?"

He said to them, "One time I rented my ass to a certain woman, and she was weeping on the way, and I said to her, 'What's with you?' and she said to me, 'The husband of that woman [me] is in prison for debt, and I wanted to see what I can do to free him.' So I sold my ass and I gave her the proceeds, and I said to her, 'Here is your money, free your husband, but do not sin by becoming a prostitute to raise the necessary funds.'"

They said to him, "You are worthy of praying and having your prayers answered."

The ass driver clearly has a powerful lien on Heaven, so that his prayers are answered, even while those of others are not. What was it he did to get that entitlement? He did what no law could demand: impoverished himself to save the woman from a fate worse than death.

⤫

In a dream of R. Abbahu, Mr. Pentakaka ("Five sins") appeared, who prayed that rain would come, and it rained. R. Abbahu sent and summoned him. He said to him, "What is your trade?"

He said to him, "Five sins does that man [I] do every day, for I am a pimp: hiring whores, cleaning up the theater, bringing home their garments for washing, dancing, and performing before them."

He said to him, "And what sort of decent thing have you ever done?"

He said to him, "One day that man [I] was cleaning the theater, and a woman came and stood behind a pillar and cried. I said to her, 'What's with you?' And she said to me, 'That woman's [my] husband is in prison, and I wanted to see what I can do to free him,' so I sold my bed and cover, and I gave the proceeds to her. I said to her, 'Here is your money, free your husband, but do not sin.'"

He said to him, "You are worthy of praying and having your prayers answered."

Yerushalmi Taanit 1:4.I

JACOB NEUSNER COMMENTS

For our sages "charity" represents an action that God wants us to do but cannot coerce us to do. It is an act of will on our part, giving to another freely and without coercion. God craves our love but he cannot command it, he can only ask for it. So states the key prayer of Judaism, "You will love the Lord your God with all your heart, with all your soul, and with all your might," as the proclamation of the Shema, the Unity of God and the faith that that unity entails. In the stories about charity that the sages of Judaism tell, giving to charity involves the belief that, just as God cannot coerce our love but yearns for it and responds to it, so we may freely do certain actions to which God will respond freely. That response, in the context of the faith, comes in the form of prayers that are answered, for example, prayers for rain in a time of drought.

Judaic Stories

A pious man from Kefar Imi appeared in a dream to the rabbis. He prayed for rain and it rained. The rabbis went up to him. His householders told them that he was sitting on a hill. They went out to him, saying to him, "Greetings," but he did not answer them.

He was sitting and eating, and he did not say to them, "You break bread too."

When he went back home, he made a bundle of faggots and put his cloak on top of the bundle instead of on his shoulder.

When he came home, he said to his household wife, "These rabbis are here because they want me to pray for rain. If I pray and it rains, it is a disgrace for them, and if not, it is a profanation of the Name of Heaven. But come, you and I will go up to the roof and pray. If it rains, we shall tell them, 'We are not worthy to pray and have our prayers answered.'"

They went up and prayed and it rained.

They came down to them and asked, "Why have the rabbis troubled themselves to come here today?"

They said to him, "We wanted you to pray so that it would rain."

He said to them, "Now do you really need my prayers? Heaven already has done its miracle."

They said to him, "Why, when you were on the hill, did we say hello to you, and you did not reply?"

He said to them, "I was then doing my job. Should I then interrupt my concentration on my work?"

They said to him, "And why, when you sat down to eat, did you not say to us, 'You break bread too'?"

He said to them, "Because I had only my small ration of bread. Why would I have invited you to eat by way of mere flattery when I knew I could not give you anything at all?"

They said to him, "And why when you came to go down, did you put your cloak on top of the bundle?"

He said to them, "Because the cloak was not mine. It was borrowed for use at prayer. I did not want to tear it."

They said to him, "And why, when you were on the hill, did your wife wear dirty clothes, but when you came down from the mountain, did she put on clean clothes?"

He said to them, "When I was on the hill, she put on dirty clothes, so that no one would gaze at her. But when I came home from the hill, she put on clean clothes, so that I would not gaze on any other woman."

They said to him, "It is well that you pray and have your prayers answered."

Taanit 1:4.I

Hillel says: Be disciples of Aaron, loving peace and pursuing peace, loving people and drawing them near to the Torah.

He would say in Aramaic: A name made great is a name destroyed, and one who does not add, subtracts.

And who does not learn is liable to death. And the one who uses the crown, passes away.

He would say: If I am not for myself, who is for me? And when I am only for myself, what am I? And if not now, when?

Loving peace: How so?

This teaches that a person should love peace among Israelites as Aaron did, as it is said: The Torah of truth was in his mouth, and unrighteousness was not found in his lips; he walked with me in peace and uprightness and did turn away many from iniquity.

Rabbi Meir says, "Why does the cited verse state: did turn away many from iniquity?

"When Aaron would go along, he might meet a bad man or a wicked one. He greeted him. The next day the same man might want to commit a transgression. But he thought to himself, 'Woe is me, how can I raise my eyes afterward and look at Aaron? I should be ashamed on his account, for he has now greeted me.' That person would then keep himself from committing a transgression.

"So too, if there were two people quarreling with each other, Aaron went and took a seat near one of them and said to him, 'My son, see your friend—what is he saying? His heart is torn, he rips his garments, saying, "Woe is me, how can I raise my eyes afterward and see my friend? I should be ashamed on his account, for I am the one who treated him foully."'

"He would sit with him until he had removed the envy from his heart.

"Then Aaron would go to his fellow and take a seat near him, and say to him, 'My son, see your friend—what is he saying? His heart is torn, he rips his garments, saying, "Woe is me, how can I raise my eyes afterward and see my friend? I should be ashamed on his account, for I am the one who treated him foully."'

"He would sit with him until he had removed the envy from his heart.

"Then, when the two met, they hugged and kissed each other.

"Therefore it is said: And every member of the house of Israel wept for Aaron for thirty days."

So too, the Holy One, blessed be he, made peace on high.

What is the peace that the Holy One, blessed be he, made on high?

That he did not call ten angels by the name of Gabriel, ten Michaels, ten Uriels, ten Raphaels, as people may use the name Reuben for ten different people, or Simeon, or Levi, or Judah.

For if he had done things the way mortals do, if he then called one of them, all of those bearing that name would come before him and express jealousy of one another.

So he called only one angel by the name of Gabriel, one Michael, and when he calls one of them, only that one comes and stands before him, and he sends him wherever he wishes.

How, then, do we know that they fear and honor one another and exhibit greater humility than do mortals?

When they open their mouths and recite a song, this one says to his fellow, "You start, for you are greater than I am," and that one says, "You start, for you are greater than I am."

This is not the way of mortals, for this one says to his fellow, "I am greater than you are," and that one says to his fellow, "I am greater than you are."

Some say that they form groups, and one group says to its fellow, "You start, for you are greater than I am."

For so it is said: "And this calls to that."

The Fathers according to Rabbi Nathan XII:I.1–IV:1

Jacob Neusner comments

A sin is what one has done by one's own volition beyond all limits of the law. So an act that generates merit for the individual is the counterpart and opposite: what one does by one's own volition that also is beyond all requirements of the law. This series of quite remarkable stories tell how unlettered men and humble women please God in ways that the most learned and holy sages are unable to do. Sages recognize that superior to their mastery of Torah is the virtue of the self-sacrificing woman and the man who helps her out.

Justice

CHAPTER 11

✠ *A Gospel Story*

Then Jesus spoke to the crowds and to his disciples. "The teachers of the Law and the Pharisees are the authorized interpreters of Moses' Law. So you must obey and follow everything they tell you to do; do not, however, imitate their actions, because they don't practice what they preach. They tie onto people's backs loads that are heavy and hard to carry, yet they aren't willing even to lift a finger to help them carry those loads. They do everything so that people will see them. Look at the straps with scripture verses on them which they wear on their foreheads and arms, and notice how large they are! Notice also how long are the tassels on their cloaks! They love the best places at feasts and the reserved seats in the synagogues; they love to be greeted with respect in the marketplaces and to have people call them 'Teacher.' You must not be called 'Teacher,' because you are all equal and have only one Teacher. And you must not call anyone here on earth 'Father,' because you have only the one Father in heaven. Nor should you be called 'Leader,' because your one and only leader is the Messiah. The greatest one among you must be your servant. Whoever makes himself great will be humbled, and whoever humbles himself will be made great."

Matthew 23:1–12

ANDREW GREELEY COMMENTS

Jesus' constant conflict with the scribes and the Pharisees was not a battle against the scribes' skills in interpreting scripture, nor with the Pharisees' theoretical doctrines about love and about the resurrection from the dead. Rather he fought with these religious enthusiasts because their claim to virtue, a claim that they used to oppress ordinary folk, was in large part hypocritical. Because they were deeply religious persons, they assumed that they had the right to run other people's lives. It was against this tyranny that Jesus contended. Patently the temptation to be a scribe or a Pharisee did not end when Jesus went back to the Father in heaven. It is an inevitable part of religion, and it must be resisted today even as it was in Jesus' time.

✠ A Christian Story

Once upon a time a young couple brought their first baby to their parish to have the small one baptized. The priest was warm and genial, welcomed them into the parish, congratulated them on their little girl, signed them up for the parish, and presided over a baptism that, because of his explanations and his dignity in the celebration, was a religious experience for all who attended. A year later a little brother appeared on the scene. The mother called the parish to arrange for the baptism. She was put through to the director of religious education (DRE), who informed her that they had to take a course for parents of children seeking baptism. The course for this semester was already underway. They would have to wait three months. Both she and her husband would have to attend on every Wednesday for six weeks or the child would not be baptized. The mother argued that both of them had received sixteen years of Catholic education, that they both worked— her husband was working on his law degree at night and had classes on Wednesday—and that she already had an infant in arms. The DRE was inflexible—no course, no baptism. "But we didn't need a course for our first child," the mother protested. "That's because I was not in charge," said the DRE, and she hung up. Who said there were no Pharisees left?

✝ *A Gospel Story*

Jesus left that place and went off to the territory near the cities of Tyre and Sidon. A Canaanite woman who lived in that region came to him. "Son of David!" she cried out. "Have mercy on me, sir! My daughter has a demon and is in a terrible condition."

But Jesus did not say a word to her. His disciples came to him and begged him, "Send her away! She is following us and making all this noise!"

Then Jesus replied, "I have been sent only to the lost sheep of the people of Israel."

At this the woman came and fell at his feet. "Help me, sir!" she said.

Jesus answered, "It isn't right to take the children's food and throw it to the dogs."

"That's true, sir," she answered, "but even the dogs eat the leftovers that fall from their masters' table."

So Jesus answered her, "You are a woman of great faith! What you want will be done for you." And at that very moment her daughter was healed.

Matthew 15:21–28

ANDREW GREELEY COMMENTS

There has been almost from the beginning of Christianity much agonizing over this text. Why was Jesus so rude to the Canaanite woman—Jesus, who was more courteous and respectful toward women than anyone of his own time about whose life we have information? However, the lesson was intended for those Jewish Christians who were uneasy about the church opening itself up to Gentiles. The dialogue probably was composed in the tradition with them in mind. However, the incident itself almost certainly goes back to the time of Jesus and was retained in the memory of the early Christians despite the fact that many thought it strange that he would be kind to a Canaanite woman. Wasn't it bad enough that he was kind to a Samaritan woman? As St. Paul would later say, there was neither Greek nor Roman, Jew nor Gentile, male nor female among the followers of Jesus, but all were one in him.

✠ *A Christian Story*

Once there was an unpopular new group in American cities. The best people in the cities said that this group was hopeless. They were slovenly, devoid of ambition, quarrelsome, drank too much, fought too much, were inclined to be brutal criminals, had too many children whom they did not know how to bring up to be proper citizens. Because of their sloppy ways and their dirtiness, they were prone to illness. They did not know how to protect the health of their children. They were a drain on the economy and the finances of the cities. The neighborhoods in which they lived were unsafe at night and often in the daylight too. They simply did not have what it takes to become good Americans. No more of them should be admitted into the country. Those who were already here should be kept in their own neighborhoods and not be permitted to live in the same communities with other Americans. They were physically, even genetically inferior. The *New York Times* said editorially that even the African Americans were not as bad as these people. Who were they? Why, the Irish of course. Who else?

🕎 *A Judaic Story*

R. Hanina bar Pappa, and some say R. Simlai, gave the following exposition of the verse, "They that fashion a graven image are all of them vanity, and their delectable things shall not profit, and their own witnesses see not nor know": "In the age to come the Holy One, blessed be he, will bring a scroll of the Torah and hold it in his bosom and say, 'Let him who has kept himself busy with it come and take his reward.' Then all the gentiles will crowd together: 'All of the nations are gathered together.' The Holy One, blessed be he, will say to them, 'Do not crowd together before me in a mob. But let each nation enter together with its scribes, "and let the peoples be gathered together," and the word "people" means "kingdom": "and one kingdom shall be stronger than the other."'

"The kingdom of Rome comes in first."

"The Holy One, blessed be he, will say to them, 'How have you defined your chief occupation?'

"They will say before him, 'Lord of the world, a vast number of marketplaces have we set up, a vast number of bathhouses we have made, a vast amount of silver and gold have we accumulated. And all of these things we have done only in behalf of Israel, so that they may define as their chief occupation the study of the Torah.'

"The Holy One, blessed be he, will say to them, 'You complete idiots! Whatever you have done has been for your own convenience. You have set up a vast number of marketplaces to be sure, but that was so as to set up whorehouses in them. The bathhouses were for your own pleasure. Silver and gold belong to me anyhow: "Mine is the silver and mine is the gold, says the Lord of hosts." Are there any among you who have been telling of "this," and "this" is only the Torah: "And this is the Torah that Moses set before the children of Israel."' So they will make their exit, humiliated.

"When the kingdom of Rome has made its exit, the kingdom of Persia enters afterward.

"The Holy One, blessed be he, will say to them, 'How have you defined your chief occupation?'

"They will say before him, 'Lord of the world, we have thrown up a vast number of bridges, we have conquered a vast number of towns, we have made a vast number of wars, and all of them we did only for Israel, so that they may define as their chief occupation the study of the Torah.'

"The Holy One, blessed be he, will say to them, 'Whatever you have done has been for your own convenience. You have thrown up a vast number of bridges, to collect tolls, you have conquered a vast number of towns, to collect the corvée, and, as to making a vast number of wars, I am the one who makes wars: "The Lord is a man of war." Are there any among you who have been telling of "this," and "this" is only the Torah: "And this is the Torah that Moses set before the children of Israel."' So they will make their exit, humiliated.

"And so it will go with each and every nation.

"They will say to him, 'Lord of the world, in point of fact, did you actually give it to us and we did not accept it?'"

But how can they present such an argument, since it is written, "The Lord came from Sinai and rose from Seir to them, he shined forth from Mount Paran," and further, "God comes from Teman." *Now what in the world did he want in Seir, and what was he looking for in Paran?* Said R. Yohanan, "This teaches that the Holy One, blessed be he, made the rounds of each and every nation and language and none accepted it, until he came to Israel, and they accepted it."

Rather, this is what they say, "Did we accept it but then not carry it out?"

But to this the rejoinder must be, "Why did you not accept it anyhow!"

Rather, "This is what they say before him, 'Lord of the world, did you hold a mountain over us like a cask and then we refused to accept it, as you did to Israel, as it is written, "And they stood beneath the mountain."'

"Then the Holy One, blessed be he, will say to them, 'Let us make known what happened first: "Let them announce to us former things." As to the seven religious duties that you did accept, where have you actually carried them out?'

"This is what the gentiles say before him, 'Lord of the world, Israel, who accepted it—where in the world have they actually carried it out?'

"The Holy One, blessed be he, will say to them, 'I shall bear witness concerning them, that they have carried out the whole of the Torah!'

"They will say before him, 'Lord of the world, is there a father who is permitted to give testimony concerning his son? For it is written, "Israel is my son, my firstborn."'

"The Holy One, blessed be he, will say to them, 'The heaven and the earth will give testimony in their behalf that they have carried out the entirety of the Torah.'

"They will say before him, 'Lord of the world, the heaven and earth have a selfish interest in the testimony that they give: "If not for my covenant with day and with night, I should not have appointed the ordinances of heaven and earth."'

"The Holy One, blessed be he, will say to them, 'Some of them may well come and give testimony concerning Israel that they have observed the entirety of the Torah. Let Nimrod come and give testimony in behalf of Abraham that he never worshiped idols. Let Laban come and give testimony in behalf of Jacob, that he never was suspect of thievery. Let the wife of Potiphar come and give testimony in behalf of Joseph, that he was never suspect of "sin." Let Nebuchadnezzar come and give testimony in behalf of Hananiah, Mishael, and Azariah, that they never bowed down to the idol. Let Darius come and give testimony in behalf of Daniel, that he did not neglect even the optional prayers. Let Bildad the Shuhite and Zophar the Naamathite and Eliphaz the Temanite and Elihu son of Barachel the Buzite come and testify in behalf of Israel that they have observed the entirety of the Torah: "Let the nations bring their own witnesses, that they may be justified."'

"They will say before him, 'Lord of the world, give it to us to begin with, and let us carry it out.'

"The Holy One, blessed be he, will say to them, 'World-class idiots! He who took the trouble to prepare on the eve of the Sabbath Friday will eat on the Sabbath, but he who took no trouble on the eve of the Sabbath—what in the world is he going to eat on the Sabbath! Still, I'll give you another chance. I have a rather simple religious duty, which is called "the tabernacle." Go and do that one.'

"Forthwith every one of them will take up the task and go and make a tabernacle on his roof. But then the Holy One, blessed be he, will come and make the sun blaze over them as at the summer solstice, and every one of them will knock down his tabernacle and go his way: 'Let us break their bands asunder and cast away their cords from us.'

"Then the Holy One, blessed be he, goes into session and laughs at them: 'He who sits in heaven laughs.'"

Talmud of Babylonia Tractate Abodah Zarah 2A–3A

JACOB NEUSNER COMMENTS

No topic more engaged the Judaic sages than justice. They conceived of God as just and merciful and aspired to imitate God in the social order that they built for holy Israel. For the sages justice applied not only to individuals but to nations, and, prizing as they did the gift of the Torah, God's self-manifestation to humanity, they sought to show why it was just on God's part to give the Torah, to begin with, to Israel in particular. Just as they held that divine justice was meted out, measure for measure, as we already have noticed, so they argued that God is just in giving the Torah to humanity through the model of holy Israel.

A Judaic Story

It has been taught on Tannaite authority:

The House of Shammai say, "There will be three groups on the Day of Judgment when the dead will rise: one comprising the thoroughly righteous, one comprising the thoroughly wicked, and one the middling people.

"The thoroughly righteous immediately are inscribed and sealed for eternal life.

"The thoroughly wicked immediately are inscribed and sealed for Gehenna, as it is written, Daniel 12:2: 'And many of those who sleep in the dust of the earth shall awake, some to eternal life and some to shame and everlasting contempt.'

"Middling people go down to Gehenna, scream in prayer, and rise again, as it is written, Zechariah 13:9: 'And I will put this third into the fire and refine them as one refines silver and test them as gold is tested. They will call on my name, and I will answer them.'

"And, concerning this group, Hannah said, 1 Samuel 2:6: 'The Lord kills and brings to life. He brings down to Sheol and raises up.'"

The Hillelites reject the notion that the middling group initially is sent to Gehenna. The House of Hillel say, "But contrary to what the Shammaites hold, God who abounds in mercy leans toward a judgment of mercy.

"And concerning them, that is, the middling group, David said, Psalm 116:1: 'I love the Lord, because he has heard my voice and my supplications.'

"And further concerning them David stated the whole passage, which begins, Psalm 116:6: 'The Lord preserves the simple; when I was brought low, he saved me.'"

Talmud of Babylonia 110b

JACOB NEUSNER COMMENTS

God's justice takes place not only in courts of law but in the workings of the everyday world. Sages did not foolishly claim that everything that happens happens for the best or that they could explain the justice of whatever takes place. But they did seek in ordinary events to uncover the workings of divine justice—and therefore also divine mercy.

Temperance

CHAPTER 12

✠ A Gospel Story

G od sent his messenger, a man named John, who came to tell people about the light, so that all should hear the message and believe. He himself was not the light; he came to tell about the light.

The Jewish authorities in Jerusalem sent some priests and Levites to John to ask him, 'Who are you?'

John did not refuse to answer, but spoke out openly and clearly, saying: "I am not the Messiah."

"Who are you, then?" they asked. "Are you Elijah?"

"No, I am not," John answered.

"Are you the Prophet?" they asked.

"No," he replied.

"Then tell us who you are," they said. "We have to take an answer back to those who sent us. What do you say about yourself?"

John answered by quoting the prophet Isaiah:

> "I am 'the voice of someone shouting in the desert:
>   Make a straight path for the Lord to travel!'"

The messengers, who had been sent by the Pharisees, then asked John, "If you are not the Messiah nor Elijah nor the Prophet, why do you baptize?"

John answered, "I baptize with water, but among you stands the one you do not know. He is coming after me, but I am not good enough even to untie his sandals."

All this happened in Bethany on the east side of the Jordan River, where John was baptizing.

John 1:6–8, 19–28

ANDREW GREELEY COMMENTS

The early Christians cast John the Baptist as a precursor of Jesus, perhaps inaccurate history but useful pedagogy, because it suggests that we too have a Baptist-like role. At another level, the Baptist had a religious insight not unlike that of Jesus. The notion of the kingdom of God, as described poetically in the psalms and the prophecies, was becoming clearer and clearer in the minds of Jewish teachers (and there were parallel developments in other religious traditions at that time). The Baptist saw the kingdom as apocalyptic and thus prepared for the appearance of Jesus' more highly developed vision.

✠ A Christian Story

Once upon a time there was a politician who was running in a close election against a clever campaigner. He had a good message and an exciting platform, but he was not well known. Thus he had to make a lot of speeches around the district, go to many meetings, attend tea parties and receptions and cocktail parties and church gatherings, and touch every possible base in the district. It was still an uphill battle. A good friend of his was his advance man, the fellow who made the arrangements for all the events and speeches and logistics for the campaign. He was not a very good advance man; rather, he was unreliable and pompous and, worst of all, disorganized. The other people in the campaign hated him, but the candidate stuck with his friend. As the election drew near, the polls showed the candidate losing ground. The advance man knew they were going to lose, so he gave up altogether. The campaign self-destructed in the last week. Yet the candidate lost by only one half of one percent of the votes. All the media people said that if the campaign had been better organized, the voters would have got to know the candidate better and he would have won in a walk.

We're supposed to be advance persons for Jesus. Sometimes you wonder why he doesn't fire us.

✠ A Gospel Story

That same day Jesus left the house and went to the lakeside, where he sat down to teach. The crowd that gathered around him was so large that he got into a boat and sat in it, while the crowd stood on the shore. He used parables to tell them many things.

"Once there was a man who went out to sow grain. As he scattered the seed in the field, some of it fell along the path, and the birds came and ate it up. Some of it fell on rocky ground, where there was little soil. The seeds soon sprouted, because the soil wasn't deep. But when the sun came up, it burned the young plants; and because the roots had not grown deep enough, the plants soon dried up. Some of the seed fell among thorn bushes, which grew up and choked the plants. But some seeds fell in good soil, and the plants bore grain: some had one hundred grains, others sixty, and others thirty."

And Jesus concluded, "Listen, then, if you have ears!"

Then the disciples came to Jesus and asked him, "Why do you use parables when you talk to the people?"

Jesus answered, "The knowledge about the secrets of the Kingdom of heaven has been given to you, but not to them. For the person who has something will be given more, so that he will have more than enough; but the person who has nothing will have taken away from him even the little he has. The reason I use parables in talking to them is that they look, but do not see, and they listen, but do not hear or understand. So the prophecy of Isaiah applies to them:

'This people will listen and listen, but not understand;
   they will look and look, but not see,
because their minds are dull,
   and they have stopped up their ears
   and have closed their eyes.
Otherwise, their eyes would see,
   their ears would hear,
   their minds would understand,
and they would turn to me, says God,
   and I would heal them.

"As for you, how fortunate you are! Your eyes see and your ears hear. I assure you that many prophets and many of God's people wanted very much to see what you see, but they could not, and to hear what you hear, but they did not.

"Listen, then, and learn what the parable of the sower means. Those who hear the message about the Kingdom but do not understand it are like the seeds that fell along the path. The Evil One comes and snatches away what was sown in them. The seeds that fell on rocky ground stand for those who receive the message gladly as soon as they hear it. But it does not sink deep into them, and they don't last long. So when trouble or persecution comes because of the message, they give up at once. The seeds that fell among thorn bushes stand for those who hear the message; but the worries about this life and the love for riches choke the message, and they don't bear fruit. And the seeds sown in the good soil stand for those who hear the message and understand it: they bear fruit, some as much as one hundred, others sixty, and others thirty."

Matthew 13:1–23

ANDREW GREELEY COMMENTS

The parables, powerful stories with a single disconcerting and challenging point, were Jesus' favorite way of teaching and, according to many scholars, reveal the religious experience of Jesus, his insight into the Father in heaven. Parables demand thought and are often hard to understand. There are two parables of the sower (which may be different versions of the same parable) that are part of a tradition of parables of reassurance, of encouragement, of confidence. They are paralleled by another tradition of parables of warning, of challenge, of urgency. The trouble with parables is that they are disturbing, baffling, puzzling. To try to explain a parable is to deprive it of its fire and fury, of its power and intensity. Even the earliest Christians, however, tried to tame the parables of Jesus. Thus the allegorical (a meaning attached to each event instead of a single powerful and disturbing meaning) interpretation of the previous story is something that Jesus, good storyteller that he was, would never have attempted. Rather, in an early stage of the Christian tradition this explanation was added to Jesus' original story. The allegory is not "wrong," but it does deprive the story today of its most powerful meaning: the word of God, God's people, God's church, God's invitation to each of us can overcome any obstacle. That is, when one thinks about it, a very disturbing notion because it demands total faith in God's word and Her eventual triumph.

✠ *A Christian Story*

Once upon a time there were two commodity brokers. One of them dashed onto the floor of the exchange and cornered the other. "Sell," he shouted, "sell!"

"Why?" his partner asked him.

"Because I've got this top secret weather report. Despite the poor beginning of the season with all the rain and the cold weather, this is going to be a bumper harvest, the biggest ever. We're going to have grain pouring out of our ears in this place." That was an odd thing to say because there never was any grain in the exchange, not these days.

The second man glanced at the weather report—it looked very official—and noted that it did indeed predict a perfect summer for the crops. If it turned out to be accurate, those who were buying grain now, going long, would lose tons of money and the short sellers could make a fortune.

"Go short! Sell now! It's a sure thing."

"Where did you get this?" his friend asked.

"Don't ask. I haven't broken any laws, but this is a sure thing. You can make a fortune!"

The second man nodded. "I see your point," he said.

"Then sell! Now!" But the second man was unwilling to take a chance. He stopped buying grain. But he didn't sell either. Then when the first crop reports came in, the bottom dropped out of the grain market. Our friend didn't lose much money but he didn't make much either. He consoled himself with the thought that one should never bet on a sure thing, even if it turns out to be sure.

A Judaic Story

There are seven traits that characterize an unformed clod, and seven a sage. (1) A sage does not speak before someone greater than he in wisdom. (2) And he does not interrupt his fellow. (3) And he is not at a loss for an answer. (4) He asks a relevant question and answers properly. (5) And he addresses each matter in its proper sequence, first, then second. (6) And concerning something he has not heard, he says, "I have not heard the answer." (7) And he concedes the truth when the other party demonstrates it. And the opposite of these traits apply to a clod.

A sage does not speak before someone greater than he in wisdom. This refers to Moses, for it is said: And Aaron spoke all the words which the Lord had spoken to Moses and did the signs in the sight of the people.

Now who was the more worthy to speak, Moses or Aaron?

One has to say it was Moses.

For Moses had heard the message from the mouth of the Almighty, while Aaron heard it from Moses.

But this is what Moses said: "Is it possible for me to speak in a situation in which my elder brother is standing?"

Therefore he said to Aaron, "Speak."

Thus it is said: And Aaron spoke all the words which the Lord had spoken to Moses.

And he does not interrupt his fellow—this refers to Aaron.

For it is said: Then Aaron spoke . . . Behold, this day have they offered their sin offering and their burnt offering . . . and such things as these have happened to me.

He kept silence until Moses had finished speaking and did not say to him, "Cut it short."

But afterward he said to Moses: Then Aaron spoke . . . Behold, this day have they offered their sin offering and their burnt offering . . . and such things as these have happened to me.

"And we are in mourning."

Some say that Aaron drew Moses apart from the group and said to him, "My brother, if of tithes, which are of lesser sanctity, it is forbidden for one who has yet to bury his deceased to eat, then a sin offering, of greater sanctity, all the more so should be forbidden as a meal to a person who has yet to bury his deceased."

Moses immediately agreed with him, as it is said: And when Moses heard it, it was well pleasing in his sight, and in the view of the Almighty as well.

He does not answer hastily. This is exemplified by Elihu ben Barachel the Buzite.

For it is said: I am young and you are very old, which is why I held back and did not tell you my opinion. I said: Days should speak, and the multitude of years should teach wisdom.

This teaches that they remained seated in silence before Job. When he stood up, they stood up. When he sat down, they sat down. When he ate, they ate. When he drank, they drank. Then he took permission from them and cursed his day:

After this Job opened his mouth and cursed his day and said: Let the day perish when I was born, and the night in which it was said, A man-child is brought forth.

Let the day perish on which my father came to my mother and she said to him, "I am pregnant."

And how do we know that they answered not out of turn? Then Job answered and said. Then answered Eliphaz the Temanite and said. Then answered Bildad the Shuhite and said. Then answered Zophar the Naamathite and said. Then Elihu the son of Barachel the Buzite answered and said:

Scripture arranged them one by one so as to let everyone in the world know that a sage does not speak before someone greater than he in wisdom. And he does not interrupt his fellow. And he does not answer hastily.

He asks a relevant question and answers properly:

This is exemplified by Judah, who said, I will be surety for him.

Not asking a relevant question is exemplified by Reuben, as it is said: And Reuben said to his father, You shall slay my two sons.

And he addresses each matter in its proper sequence, first, then second:

This is exemplified by Jacob.

And some say, this is exemplified by Sarah. Second, this is exemplified by the men of Haran. And he concedes the truth:

This is exemplified by Moses: And the Lord said to me, They have said well that which they have spoken.

It is further exemplified by the Holy One, blessed be he: The Lord spoke to Moses, saying, The daughters of Zelophehad speak right.

> The Fathers according to Rabbi Nathan XXXVII:XI–XVII

JACOB NEUSNER COMMENTS

Sages cultivated the virtue of temperance, by which they meant a variety of specific qualities. First and foremost, to be temperate is to practice wisdom, meaning, all things in moderation and with foresight and insight. To be temperate is to listen to the other and respond to the point of the other. It is to practice civility and good manners. While, therefore, temperance is commonly understood to refer to not drinking too much, the category encompasses most of the social virtues.

These distillations of commonsense wisdom make possible the good life among thoughtful people. The traits in the above story reveal the temperate person as one who is thoughtful and moderate.

▣ A Judaic Story

Say little and do much: How so?

This teaches that righteous people say little but do much, while wicked people say much and even a little bit they scarcely accomplish.

How do we know that righteous people say little but do much?

We find in the case of our father, Abraham, that he said to the angels, "You shall eat bread with me today," for it is said: And I will fetch a morsel of bread and satisfy your hunger.

But in the end see what Abraham did for the ministering angels! He went and prepared for them three oxen and nine seahs of fine flour.

So too the Holy One, blessed be he, said little but did much.

For it is said: And the Lord said to Abram, Know with certainty that your seed will be a stranger in a land that does not belong to them and shall serve them and they shall afflict them four hundred years and also that nation whom they shall serve will I punish and afterward they shall come out with great substance.

He said to them only that he would punish them by means of his name, "the Lord." But in the end, when the Holy One, blessed be he, exacted punishment from Israel, he exacted punishment only with the name of seventy-two letters.

For it is said: Or has God tried to go and take for himself a nation from the midst of another nation, by trials, by signs, and by wonders . . . and by great terrors.

Lo, we learn that when the Holy One, blessed be he, exacted punishment from Israel, he exacted punishment only with the name of seventy-two letters.

The Fathers according to Rabbi Nathan XIII:I–II

JACOB NEUSNER COMMENTS

Wisdom knows the difference between boasting and actually doing, and honors those who don't promise but deliver. That is the highest virtue: temperance in words, extravagance in accomplishment.

Fortitude

CHAPTER 13

✠ A Gospel Story

Jesus said, "A person is born physically of human parents, but is born spiritually of the Spirit. Do not be surprised because I tell you that you must all be born again. The wind blows wherever it wishes; you hear the sound it makes, but you do not know where it comes from or where it is going. It is like that with everyone who is born of the Spirit."

"How can this be?" asked Nicodemus.

Jesus answered, "You are a great teacher in Israel, and you don't know this? I am telling you the truth: we speak of what we know and report what we have seen, yet none of you is willing to accept our message. You do not believe me when I tell you about the things of this world; how will you ever believe me, then, when I tell you about the things of heaven? And no one has ever gone up to heaven except the Son of Man, who came down from heaven.

"As Moses lifted up the bronze snake on a pole in the desert, in the same way the Son of Man must be lifted up, so that everyone who believes in him may have eternal life. For God loved the world so much that he gave his only Son, so that everyone who believes in him may not die but have eternal life. For God did not send his Son into the world to be its judge, but to be its savior.

"Those who believe in the Son are not judged; but those who do not believe have already been judged, because they have not believed in God's only Son."

John 3:6–18

ANDREW GREELEY COMMENTS

The doctrine of the Holy Trinity was not revealed to baffle us, to test us, to challenge our faith. Rather, it discloses to us that there is so much knowledge and so much love in God that it flows over into different personalities. God is necessarily a community of knowledge, power, and love. If a God like that is on our side, what do we have to be afraid of? The doctrine of the Trinity is for our reassurance and consolation. This Gospel story echoes this theme: it depicts Jesus telling his disciples that there is nothing to fear, even if he is about to leave them. He and the Father and the Spirit will continue to protect them. He does not guarantee that there will not be trouble or suffering, but he does promise that there will be victory and eternal life.

✠ *A Christian Story*

Once upon a time there was a sophomore basketball team that was, to tell the truth, somewhat less skilled than the Chicago Bulls. Or so it seemed. They couldn't shoot very well, their passing was sloppy, they almost never got a rebound, they didn't hustle, and, worst of all, they knew they were no good. Then they got a new coach and two new assistants who volunteered to help them.

"You are going to take city," the coach said. "You are the most talented group of young women your age I have ever seen. There is no reason why you can't beat everyone."

They laughed.

The three coaches stared at them sternly. "No more laughing," the head coach said. "Now the first thing we are going to do is practice free throws. Young women as good as you are should make nine out of ten free throws. We'll accept nothing less."

"Shaq shoots less than fifty percent," one of the kids said.

"You're better than Shaq," the coach replied.

Well, you know what? The coach was right. Inspired by the coaching staff's confidence and experience, and with their skills honed by lots of practice and hard work, they did win city. They were the greatest. Or at least with that threesome on their side, they came to believe they were the greatest, which was all that mattered.

✠ *A Gospel Story*

In the sixth month of Elizabeth's pregnancy God sent the angel Gabriel to a town in Galilee named Nazareth. He had a message for a young woman promised in marriage to a man named Joseph, who was a descendant of King David. Her name was Mary. The angel came to her and said, "Peace be with you! The Lord is with you and has greatly blessed you!"

Luke 1:26–28

ANDREW GREELEY COMMENTS

Father Raymond Brown in his masterful book on the infancy narratives says that these stories are "theologumena," not so much literal history but stories with a theological point—the gratuitous and revolutionary impact of Jesus' birth, life, and death. It is perhaps not necessary to fixate on this point. People love the Christmas stories because of their beauty and hopefulness and excitement. In fact, we do not know how they were put together or where they come from or how they got into the Gospels. It is certainly not forbidden to think that there might be a good deal more history in them than we are able to prove. But the important point is that they are stories of God's love and of Jesus' role in history and that's what counts, not historical details. One element is literally true, however. The storyteller puts on Mary's lips the totally accurate prediction (which perhaps the real Mary would not have dared to say) that all nations would call her blessed. They sure have.

✠ A Christian Story

Once upon a time there was a woman who hated children. She had been raised in a large family where there were constant fights between the parents, between parents and children, and among the children. She did not want to be any part of a family like that ever again in her life. Kids were noisy, obnoxious brats. They were messy, ungrateful, dishonest. From the moment of conception till you finally got rid of them when you sent them off to college, they caused nothing but pain. And they fought with you for the rest of your life and broke your heart. Her friends who had children said that her picture of children was incomplete. They were also wonderful, even if they were often pesky brats. Her husband wanted children desperately, but she told him that if he wanted them so much, he should find himself another wife. Well, one day she found that something had gone wrong and she was pregnant. She instantly thought about having an abortion to get rid of the child before anyone found out about it. She hesitated.

"You ought to take a chance with the kid," one of her friends—the only to whom she had told the bad news—advised her.

She even went to see a doctor about an abortion, but then she changed her mind at the last minute and decided to take a chance.

"Every woman who ever becomes pregnant takes a chance," her friend said.

Well, you know what happened. You would think she had invented motherhood! Moreover, she was a very good mother and did not repeat the mistakes of the family in which she was raised. Her children adored her.

Mary took a chance, too, not utterly different from the one every mother takes. That is the nature of life, of responding to the kingdom, to seize the rich opportunities it offers us.

♆ A Judaic Story

Our rabbis have taught on Tannaite authority:

When R. Eleazar b. Parta and R. Hanina b. Teradion were arrested, R. Eleazar b. Parta said to R. Hanina b. Teradion, "You are fortunate, for you have been arrested on only one count. Woe is me, that I have been arrested on five counts."

Said to him R. Hanina, "You are fortunate, for you have been arrested on five counts but you will be saved, while woe is me, for although I have been arrested on only one count, I will not be rescued. For you have devoted yourself to the study of the Torah and also acts of beneficence, while I devoted myself only to the study of the Torah."

They brought R. Eleazar b. Parta and said to him, "How come you have repeated Mishnah traditions and how come you have been a thief?"

He said to them, "If a thief, then not a scribe, and if a scribe, then not a thief, and as I am not the one, so I am not the other."

"Then how come they call you 'rabbi'?"

"I am the rabbi of the weavers."

They brought him two coils of wool and asked, "Which is the warp and which is the woof?"

A miracle happened, and a she-bee came and sat on the warp and a he-bee came and sat on the woof, so he said, "This is the warp and that is the woof."

They said to him, "And how come you didn't come to the temple of idolatry [literally: house of destruction] to worship?"

He said to them, "I am an elder, and I was afraid that people would trample me under their feet."

"And up to now how many old people have been trampled?"

A miracle happened, and on that very day an old man was trampled.

"And how come you freed your slave?"

He said to them, "No such thing took place."

One of them was about to get up to give testimony against him, when Elijah came and appeared to him in the form of one of the important lords of the government and said to that man, "Just as miracles were done for him in all other matters, a miracle is going to happen in this one, and you will turn out to be a common scold."

But he paid no attention to him and got up to address them, and a letter from important members of the government had to be sent to the Caesar, and it was through that man that it was sent; on the road Elijah came and threw him four hundred parasangs, so he went and never came back.

They brought R. Hanina b. Teradion and said to him, "How come you devoted yourself to the Torah?"

He said to them, "It was as the Lord my God has commanded me."

Forthwith they made the decree that he was to be put to death by burning, his wife to be killed, and his daughter to be assigned to a whorehouse.

He was sentenced to be burned to death, for he had pronounced the Divine Name as it is spelled out.

And why was his wife sentenced to be put to death? Because she did not stop him.

And why was his daughter sentenced to a whorehouse? For, said R. Yohanan, "One time his daughter was walking before the great authorities of Rome. They said, 'How beautiful are the steps of this maiden,' and she forthwith became meticulous about her walk."

When three of them went out, they accepted the divine decree. He said, "The rock, his work is perfect, for all his ways are justice."

His wife said, "A God of faithfulness and without iniquity, just and right is he.

His daughter said, "Great in counsel and mighty in deed, whose eyes are open on all the ways of the sons of men, to give everyone according to his ways and according to the fruit of his deeds.

Said Rabbi [Judah the Patriarch], "How great are these righteous. For it was for their sake in particular that these verses, which justify God's judgment, were made ready for the moment of the acceptance of God's judgment."

Mishnah Eduyyot 5:6

JACOB NEUSNER COMMENTS

Holy Israel's long history of suffering to remain loyal to God made manifest in the Torah yields a vast, sad corpus of stories of courage, self-sacrifice, and martyrdom—the three components of fortitude. For our sages the record of their own martyrs, who proclaimed God's unity even from the pyre, defined the meaning of courage.

A Judaic Story

When Isaac was old, and his eyes were dim, so that he could not see, he called Esau his older son, and said to him, "My son," and he answered, "Here I am."

Said R. Judah bar Simon, "Abraham sought the physical traits of old age so that from his appearance, people would know that he was old. He said before him, 'Lord of all ages, when a man and his son come in somewhere, no one knows whom to honor. If you crown a man with the traits of old age, people will know whom to honor.'

"Said to him the Holy One, blessed be he, 'By your life, this is a good thing that you have asked for, and it will begin with you.'

"From the beginning of the book of Genesis to this passage, there is no reference to old age. But when Abraham our father came along, the traits of old age were given to him, as it is said: 'And Abraham was old.'

"Isaac asked God for suffering. He said before him, 'Lord of the age, if someone dies without suffering, the measure of strict justice is stretched out against him. But if you bring suffering on him, the measure of strict justice will not be stretched out against him. Suffering will help counter the man's sins, and the measure of strict justice will be mitigated through suffering by the measure of mercy.'

"Said to him the Holy One, blessed be he, 'By your life, this is a good thing that you have asked for, and it will begin with you.'

"From the beginning of the book of Genesis to this passage, there is no reference to suffering. But when Isaac came along, suffering was given to him: 'His eyes were dim.'

"Jacob asked for sickness. He said before him, 'Lord of all ages, if a person dies without illness, he will not settle his affairs for his children. If he is sick for two or three days, he will settle his affairs with his children.'

"Said to him the Holy One, blessed be he, 'By your life, this is a good thing that you have asked for, and it will begin with you.'

"That is in line with this verse: 'And someone said to Joseph, "Behold, your father is sick."'

Said R. Levi, "Abraham introduced the innovation of old age, Isaac introduced the innovation of suffering, Jacob introduced the innovation of sickness.

"Hezekiah introduced the innovation of chronic illness. He said to him, 'You have kept a man in good condition until the day he dies. But if someone is sick and gets better, he will carry out a complete and sincere act of repentance for his sins.'

"Said to him the Holy One, blessed be he, 'By your life, this is a good thing that you have asked for, and it will begin with you.'

"The writing of Hezekiah, king of Judah, when he had been sick and recovered of his sickness."

Said R. Samuel b. Nahman, "On the basis of that verse we know that between one illness and another there was an illness more serious than either one."

Genesis Rabbah LXV:IX

JACOB NEUSNER COMMENTS

From every person fortunate enough to grow old, fortitude is asked. For old age, suffering, and sickness are not for the weak. But in the Torah these are gifts from God, prayed for by the founders of the world, Abraham, Isaac, and Jacob. What is natural to the human condition we must not only accept but affirm. What is part of life forms a gift that comes to us with life, and fortitude transforms old age, suffering, and sickness into our offering of thanks to God for life.

Prudence

CHAPTER 14

✛ *A Gospel Story*

Jesus told them another parable: "The Kingdom of heaven is like this. A man sowed good seed in his field. One night, when everyone was asleep, an enemy came and sowed weeds among the wheat and went away. When the plants grew and the heads of grain began to form, then the weeds showed up.

"The man's servants came to him and said, 'Sir, it was good seed you sowed in your field; where did the weeds come from?' 'It was some enemy who did this,' he answered. 'Do you want us to go and pull up the weeds?' they asked him. 'No,' he answered, 'because as you gather the weeds you might pull up some of the wheat along with them. Let the wheat and the weeds both grow together until harvest. Then I will tell the harvest workers to pull up the weeds first, tie them in bundles and burn them, and then to gather in the wheat and put it in my barn.'"

Jesus told them another parable: "The Kingdom of heaven is like this. A man takes a mustard seed and sows it in his field. It is the smallest of all seeds, but when it grows up, it is the biggest of all plants. It becomes a tree, so that birds come and make their nests in its branches."

Jesus told them still another parable: "The Kingdom of heaven is like this. A woman takes some yeast and mixes it with a bushel of flour until the whole batch of dough rises."

Matthew 13:24–33

ANDREW GREELY COMMENTS

This parable is in all probability a "doubling" of a prior parable in St. Matthew. He found both of them in the tradition with which he was working. They were sufficiently different for him to include both in his Gospel. The mustard seed story is an addition in this version. It turns out to be an accurate prediction. Sociologist Rodney Stark in a recent study argues that there were only a thousand Christians at the end of the first century, six million at the beginning of the third, and thirty million (half the Roman empire) by 350. Constantine's conversion, he suggests, was a result of the growth of Christianity, not its cause.

✠ A Christian Story

Once upon a time there was an eighth-grade football team that inherited a tradition of losing almost all the games of a season. The other parishes in the league provided uniforms, a coaching staff, even summer training for their teams. The kids from St. Useless didn't have a coach or uniforms or much parental support. They were a ragtag band of talented but untrained kids. Then one day a young man watched them stumble through practice.

"Can I help?" he asked them.

The team was ready to accept help from anyone.

"You guys are the best," he said. "There's no reason you can't win the conference. But you have to practice, be confident of yourself, and be good friends. No more fighting among the team or with me if I'm going to be your unofficial coach."

The kids agreed. The first thing the coach taught them was how to be friends and play together. Then he told them practice after practice how good they were. Finally he made them work, work, work.

You know what happened. They went undefeated and won the conference.

"He made us believe in ourselves," the kids said.

The next year the parents hired a "real coach" and the team finished last.

✠ A Gospel Story

This is the Good News about Jesus Christ, the Son of God. It began as the prophet Isaiah had written:

> "God said, 'I will send my my messenger ahead of you
>   to open the way for you.'
> Someone is shouting in the desert,
>   'Get the road ready for the Lord;
>   make a straight path for him to travel!'"

So John appeared in the desert, baptizing and preaching. "Turn away from your sins and be baptized," he told the people, "and God will forgive your sins." Many people from the province of Judea and the city of Jerusalem went out to hear John. They confessed their sins, and he baptized them in the Jordan River.

John wore clothes made of camel's hair, with a leather belt around his waist, and his food was locusts and wild honey. He announced to the people, "The man who will come after me is much greater than I am. I am not good enough even to bend down and untie his sandals. I baptize you with water, but he will baptize you with the Holy Spirit."

Mark 1:1–8

ANDREW GREELEY COMMENTS

The early Christians had a problem with the Baptist. He had preached the nearness of the kingdom of God before Jesus had. And Jesus had been baptized by him. Thus the Baptist's disciples could claim that their master was prior to and therefore superior to the master of the Christians. So the Christians rearranged history a little bit for pedagogical purposes. The Baptist was not so much preaching about an apocalyptic intervention of God that would punish all sinners as he was preaching about the coming of Jesus who would embody the kingdom of God. In fact, the kingdom as preached by Jesus was a kingdom of love and mercy lurking near to and all around humankind, a difference that is perhaps more important today than it seemed to the early Christians.

✠ *A Christian Story*

Once upon a time there was a company that was in a bad way. The last three CEOs had been dummies. The company's stock had lost 60 percent of its value, its market share had declined by 30 percent, its bright people were leaving, morale among the employees was at rock bottom. The worst part of the trouble was that the product they made was still the best in the market. But the previous leaders had been lazy and mean and had spent most of their time awarding themselves and their friends huge bonuses. They paid no attention to advertising or marketing. Finally a new board was appointed at the stockholders' insistence. They fired the last CEO with a thunderous denunciation. They warned the employees that all their jobs— and their pensions—were in grave jeopardy. The workers were terrified. Finally the new CEO arrived. He was expected to fire half the workers, cut back on expenses, and give the company the good shaking that everyone said it needed. Instead he walked around the building, smiled at everyone, assured them that everyone would be all right and that he didn't plan to fire anyone.

"Another fool" they said.

Then he met with the union leaders to get their suggestions. They told him the truth: that the product was the best in the business.

"I thought that too," he said. Then he hired a new marketing and advertising director, brought in a new advertising and public relations firm, and launched a very clever television campaign. By that time everyone in the company admired him and worked hard for him. In six months the company was well on the way to recovery.

"You catch more flies with honey," a top executive said of him. And added, mixing his metaphors, "some nice guys finish first."

And the new boss merely said, "The fear of the Lord is the beginning of wisdom, but only the beginning."

🕎 *A Judaic Story*

"Even in your thought do not curse the king, nor in your bedchamber curse the rich; for a bird of the air will carry your voice, or some winged creature tell the matter."

Said R. Abin, "God says, 'You should not curse and blaspheme before me with that very capacity for thought that I gave you beyond what I gave to domesticated beasts, wild animals, and fowl.

"'For you I created two eyes and for them two eyes, for you two ears and for them two ears. I made you like them. Yet to him, namely, to man, they must keep silent.

"'He is like the beasts that keep silent.' God speaks: 'I have silenced them on account of the honor owing to you.'

"'How many favors have I done for you, and yet you do not understand.' 'Man in his honor does not understand.'"

"Nor in your bedchamber curse the rich." Do not curse the rich man who thrives in your own generation.

"For a bird of the air will carry your voice."

Said R. Levi, "There is a voice that goes forth for good and there is a voice that goes forth for evil.

"There is a voice that goes forth for good: 'And the Lord heard the voice of your speaking, when you spoke to me, and the Lord said to me, "They have spoken well in all that they have said."'

Levi resumes his discourse: "There is a voice that goes forth for evil: 'And the Lord heard all the voice of your words and he grew angry.'"

R. Hama in the name of R. Tahalipa, his father-in-law, said, "The Holy One, blessed be he, said, 'To you it appears to be anger, but to me it does not appear to be anger.'

"'Wherefore I swore in my anger.' 'In my anger I swore, but I retract.'

"'If they shall come to my rest.' 'To this rest they will not come, but they shall come to another rest in the age to come.'"

R. Levi in the name of Bar Qappara said, "The matter may be compared to the case of a king who grew angry with his son and made a decree that he might not join him in his palace.

"What did the king then do when he regretted his wrathful oath? He went and tore down the palace and rebuilt it and brought his son to live with him in the new palace.

"Thus he turned out to carry out his original oath and at the same time to bring his son in.

"So said the Holy One, blessed be he, 'Wherefore I swore in my anger that they should not enter into my rest.'

"To this rest they will not enter, but they will enter another rest.

"For a bird of the air will carry your voice or some winged creature tell the matter."

Said R. Abin, "When a man sleeps, the body tells it to the soul, the soul to the spirit, the spirit to the angel, the angel to the cherub, the cherub to the winged creature, and the winged creature will tell the matter before him who spoke and brought the world into being."

Leviticus Rabbah XXXII:II.1ff.

JACOB NEUSNER COMMENTS

Prudence, like temperance and fortitude, covers a range of specific attitudes and actions. To start with, to be prudent is to watch what one says. We do not have to say everything we think, and we often do well to look for the right time to tell the truth.

🕎 *A Judaic Story*

"And your ancient ruins shall be rebuilt."

R. Tarfon gave to R. Aqiba six silver centenarii, saying to him, "Go, buy us a piece of land, so we can get a living from it and labor in the study of Torah together."

He took the money and handed it out to scribes, Mishnah teachers, and those who study Torah.

After some time R. Tarfon met him and said to him, "Did you buy the land that I mentioned to you?"

He said to him, "Yes."

He said to him, "Is it any good?"

He said to him, "Yes."

He said to him, "And do you not want to show it to me?"

He took him and showed him the scribes, Mishnah teachers, and people who were studying Torah, and the Torah that they had acquired. He said to him, "Is there anyone who works for nothing? Where is the deed covering the field?"

He said to him, "It is with King David, concerning whom it is written, 'He has scattered, he has given to the poor, his righteousness endures for ever.'"

Leviticus Rabbah XXXIV:XVI

JACOB NEUSNER COMMENTS

Prudence involves careful management of one's material resources, along with a clear notion of what really matters. For the sages of the Torah, economics—the rational disposition of scarce resources—extended to matters other than material resources. In their day real estate represented truly secure wealth, but they explicitly defined scarce resources in a different way and advised prudent management of the truly scarce resource, which is learning in the Torah. In this famous story, people understand by "wealth" the material things of the world. But wisdom defines wealth differently. Specifically, the story has one sage identify wealth with silver and gold and especially real estate, while the other explains that true wealth is learning, specifically in this setting, study of the Torah.

Conclusion

Telling the Same Story in Different Ways

MARY GREELEY DURKIN

T he rabbi and the priest tell their stories of faith. In so doing, they invite us to join their quest for a common ground, for a shared vision, that speaks to the search for meaning in our contemporary world. The stories they tell, from the perspective of Rabbinic Judaism and Catholic Christianity, though often very different, share an underlying vision of the God/human relationship. Though they make no claim to theological dialogue, their vision is rooted in an understanding of that relationship, confirming their belief in the same God.

A caveat before we turn to that vision as it emerges in their storytelling: As in any anthology with a common theme, the stories challenge the reader to uncover the many levels of meaning that emerge from the stories. The readers bring to the stories their own experiences and often discover different meanings in the stories. Having acknowledged that, I join in this dialogue from the perspective of a theologian, searching for ways to bridge the gap that theology encounters in Jewish-Christian dialogue.

As they swap tales from their respective traditions, the rabbi and the priest address the common human search for meaning. They find, as their stories illustrate, sometimes directly, sometimes obliquely, that this search finds direction when supported by a belief in a creator God who continues to be involved with us, promising love and support even when condemning certain behaviors. The experiences of Sinai for Judaism and of Easter for the Christian are the reference points that ground each tradition's belief. The stories elaborate on the implications of these experiences for believers.

Men and women in the time of rabbinic Judaism and early Christianity and in the present time continually face the questions of meaning. Though we might ignore the need to address this quest, the deep longings of the human heart surface as we struggle to do good (be virtuous) and shun evil (avoid vices). People often disagree on what is good and what is evil. Few would deny that some behaviors edify and some shock, and some experiences cry out for explanations. The stories the rabbi and priest tell of virtues and vices illustrate the communality of our ongoing, internal struggle with vice and virtue.

The encounters with these behaviors give pause even to the most vocal unbeliever. Those who believe in the God of Sinai and the God of Easter find answers to the search for meaning in their relationship with their God, a relationship discovered in the stories of that relationship often acquired at an early age.

The images of God passed on to us through stories influence whether we opt for the vision of life as meaningful or meaningless. The young boy asking why this night is special and the young girl gazing at the Christmas crèche absorb an image of God and their relationship to God that influences them much more than most of the formal religious education they encounter later in life.

The tales in this dialogue are tales of faith. At the same time, they are tales of God and of the God/human relationship. As they address the various behaviors that contribute to harmonious living (virtues) and those that destroy human relationships (vices), the stories challenge believers to pay attention to how their faith influences their actions. The stories told by the rabbi and the priest suggest that a faith perspective challenges and supports us as we seek the good and avoid the evil.

Even the most virtuous person admits to behavior that is sinful, and the admitted sinner oftentimes surprises with acts of virtue. The reasons we sin are varied. Some blame the fall; others claim it is part of human nature. More often than not we sin because of our own insecurities, fear of ridicule, fear of death, and failure to admit that there are questions of meaning.

We do the evil we would not wish to do as an attempt to fill the void we experience when life seems—sometimes momentarily, at others times for sustained periods—meaningless. Surprisingly, even when we act out of a sense of hopelessness, most people aspire to virtue. Indeed, sometimes we fool ourselves into believing that our sinful behavior is virtuous.

Virtue inspires us and our virtuous behavior sustains us. We are confirmed in our belief that life is good and has meaning. The promise that our God loves us and is with us supports our attempts to lead good lives. This promise also challenges us when we fall victim to the attractions of vices, the cardinal sins. Contemporary Jews and Christians share a belief in this promise. This shared belief invites them to work together to address the problems that confront our world, many of which are rooted in the loss of a sense of ultimate meaning.

This swapping of tales illustrates how storytelling dialogue is an ongoing, never-ending process. The priest and rabbi tell their stories. As they listen to each other, and as we listen to both of them, new understandings of the other emerge. At the same time, we discover stories of our own that speak of the God/human story. The common ground that unites us in our search is found in our shared belief in a God who lives and acts in human history.

The new stories provide additional insights. They tell how God's love has inspired us and others to overcome adversity, to triumph over sin and practice virtue. We are invited to share our stories with others. When we share stories, we begin to share at the imaginative level. There we find the inspiration to imagine how things might be better for us and our world.

We engage in this God/human storytelling for the same reason that the sleepy child wanting a few more minutes of adult attention says, "Tell me a story." We don't add, as the child does, "And then I'll go to bed." However, we, like the child, look for the assurance that somehow all is right with our world. The God discovered in our religious tales promises us that, in the long run, we have that assurance. The stories invite us to live out of that vision.

Let the dialogue continue and be fruitful.